The Architecture of Additions

DESIGN AND REGULATION

The Architecture of Additions

DESIGN AND REGULATION

PAUL SPENCER BYARD

W. W. NORTON & COMPANY
NEW YORK • LONDON

For information about permission to reproduce
selections from this book, write to Permissions,
W. W. Norton & Company, 500 Fifth Avenue,
New York, NY 10110.

The text of this book is composed in New Baskerville
with the display set in Futura

Manufacturing by Quebecor
Book design by Abigail Sturges
Cover photograph: Dennis Gilbert / VIEW

Library of Congress Cataloging-in-Publication Data
Byard, Paul Spencer
The architecture of additions : design and regulation
/ Paul Spencer Byard.
p. cm.
Includes index.
ISBN 0-393-73021-2
1. Building—Additions. 2. Architecture—Aesthetics. 3.
Architecture—Decision making. I. Title
NA2500.B93   1998   98-10361   98-1036
720'.1—dc21   CIP

ISBN 0-393-73021-2

W. W. Norton & Company Inc., 500 Fifth Avenue,
New York, NY 10110
http://www.wwnorton.com
W. W. Norton & Company Ltd., 10 Coptic Street,
London WC1A 1PU

0 9 8 7 6 5 4 3 2 1

CONTENTS

Preface 9

Introduction: The Public Worth of Architectural Expression 10

1. The Evolution of Expression in Combined Works:
Lessons from the Masters 16

SAINT PETER'S CHURCH 18
THE QUEEN'S HOUSE AND THE GREENWICH ROYAL NAVAL HOSPITAL 21
THE CASTELVECCHIO 25

2. Twentieth-Century Combined Works:
The Expressive Possibilities of Modernism 30

Extension 32

GÖTEBURG LAW COURTS 32
YALE UNIVERSITY ART GALLERY 36
ALLEN MEMORIAL ART MUSEUM 39
MUSEUM OF DECORATIVE ARTS 43
MUSEUM FOR PRE- AND EARLY HISTORY 46
FALKESTRASSE 6 48
ING BANK 49

Derivation 50

MAISON DE VERRE 50
HUBERTUS HOUSE 53
500 PARK AVENUE 54
THE MAISON CARRÉE AND THE CARRÉ D'ART 57
IRCAM 60

Transformation 64

CENTRE POMPIDOU 65
LOUVRE PYRAMID, PALAIS DU LOUVRE 67
LYON OPERA HOUSE 70
THE REICHSTAG 72

3. Twentieth-century Combined Works and the Law:
The Special Case of "Preservation" 76

The Legal Background 77

A Test for Preservation 84

The Protected Identity and Its Place in the New Hierarchy 85

LAMBS' CLUB 85
UNITED STATES CUSTOM HOUSE 87
NEW YORK MERCHANTS' EXCHANGE 88

Securing the Place of the Protected Identity 91

NAUMBERG BAND SHELL, CENTRAL PARK 91
NUMBER ONE POULTRY LANE 95
KIMBELL ART MUSEUM 99
DOWNING COLLEGE: THE MAITLAND ROBINSON LIBRARY 102
DANA CENTER, CENTRAL PARK 105

Protecting Particular Sources of Identity 105

Façades and Façadomy 105

SECOND BRANCH BANK OF THE UNITED STATES 106
PENN MUTUAL LIFE INSURANCE COMPANY 108

Plans 110

UNIVERSITY OF VIRGINIA 110
SALK INSTITUTE 114

Master Plans 116

SHERMAN FAIRCHILD CENTER FOR THE LIFE SCIENCES, COLUMBIA UNIVERSITY 117
BROOKLYN MUSEUM OF ART 121

Building Types 124

FITZWILLIAM COLLEGE CHAPEL 124
SAINT JOHN'S COLLEGE LIBRARY 126
CATHEDRAL CHURCH OF SAINT JOHN THE DIVINE 128

Adding On 131

THE OCTAGON 131
SAINSBURY WING, NATIONAL GALLERY 135
WHIG AND CLIO 137
IL MAGISTERO 139
BRACKEN HOUSE 140
GUGGENHEIM MUSEUM 142
WASHINGTON COURT, GREENWICH VILLAGE 145
SEAMEN'S CHURCH INSTITUTE AND 250 WATER STREET, SOUTH STREET SEAPORT 147

Adding Over 151

WHITNEY MUSEUM OF AMERICAN ART 151
NEW-YORK HISTORICAL SOCIETY 153
METROPOLITAN CLUB 155
GRAND CENTRAL TERMINAL 156

4. Combined Works and Contemporary Expression:
The Architecture of Additions at the End of the Twentieth Century   160

The Architecture of Imitation   161

Architecture in the Shape of Things   163

WEXNER CENTER FOR THE VISUAL ARTS   164
FRED AND GINGER   166
JEWISH WING, BERLIN MUSEUM   167
THE BOILERHOUSE, VICTORIA AND ALBERT MUSEUM   168

The Architecture of Appropriateness   168

JEROME M. GREENE HALL, COLUMBIA LAW SCHOOL   169
JEWETT ARTS CENTER AND THE DAVIS MUSEUM AND CULTURAL CENTER   171
PALAIS DES BEAUX ARTS   172

The Architecture of Possibility   174

STUDIO NATIONAL DES ARTS CONTEMPORAINS   175
HISTORY AND LAW FACULTIES, CAMBRIDGE UNIVERSITY   177
LINGOTTO CONFERENCE CENTER   179

Afterword: The Architecture of Additions   182

Acknowledgments   183

Photo Credits   184

Index   187

The addition proposed by Marcel Breuer's office for Grand Central Terminal in 1968

The exploration pursued in this book began in an effort to understand what's wrong with the picture of Grand Central Terminal shown on the facing page. Something clearly was wrong with the slab that Penn Central Railroad proposed to add on top; the city of New York forbade its construction and the United States Supreme Court upheld the city's action. In the act, an evil was prevented that seemed as serious as the demolition of Pennsylvania Station a few years before.

The issue was a subtle one. Grand Central was conceived as Terminal City, the focus of a very dense urban center. The infrastructure in and around it made its location priceless for office development. The Terminal itself was designed to have a large tower over it; foundations and provisions for future elevators were built in. An elevation for a tower had existed for years. Over time, as towers rose around it, Grand Central was left at the bottom of a pit. Just before the Penn Central proposal, the huge slab of Pietro Belluschi's Pan Am building was built astride Grand Central's tracks. Over the Terminal the remaining hole called out to be filled.

The issue thus was not practical; it was aesthetic. Something was wrong not with what the railroad's building proposed to do—the functional issues raised by adding offices over the Terminal—but with the building's expression—what Marcel Breuer's design proposed to say from its position above the Terminal and, more particularly, what it proposed to say when read together with what the Terminal was already saying down below.

The issue, that is, had to do with the ultimate value of the proposal as architecture, with the meaning it expressed as a work of art. The issue more precisely had to do with that expression when read with the expression of its older neighbor. How does one building affect the meaning of another when their expressions are combined and

An alternative proposal from before 1915

interact? How should they affect each other when one of them is protected in the public interest?

The first question is ideally the basic business of every thoughtful design of an addition to an old building. The second question, given its consequences, has a special public importance. The Penn Central example stands for the proposition that an addition that says the wrong thing to a protected neighbor can be forbidden, a serious consequence indeed. When in fairness is that consequence the right consequence? How can it be avoided?

This book suggests a framework for answering both questions. It offers its proposals in the hope that they may help architects work successfully with significant buildings and, as important, help interested private and public persons understand their work and arrive at judgments about success and failure that are rational, satisfying, and enforceable.

The Public Worth of Architectural Expression

The architecture of Mount Vernon is preserved for what it says about George Washington

Thomas Walter's new dome for the United States Capitol reflects the emerging might of the nation in 1855

The public worth of architecture resides partly in what buildings do, in the functional support they provide for our lives, and partly in what buildings say, the understandings they display publicly and for long periods of time about ourselves, our capacities, and our purposes as human beings. The second aspect of the worth of architecture—the worth of its meaning—derives from the inescapable entanglement of architecture with expression. Anything built inevitably says something about what it is doing, about those involved in it, and about their view of the world. That it should say something worth listening to is an integral part of the discipline architecture sets for itself as an art. Buildings succeed as architecture only to the extent they simultaneously do well what they are asked to do and say something interesting and satisfying about the human condition. The resulting expressions of meaning have public value not just for the pleasure of it: the displays buildings make of ourselves to ourselves are among our most important public opportunities to learn.

The public worth of what architecture does is recognized in laws expressing public interests in how buildings function, setting and enforcing standards for safety and similar matters. The public worth of what architecture says is also recognized by law, most importantly by laws expressing public interests in historic preservation. These laws seek to protect particularly valuable understandings about the human condition expressed by existing architecture and to ensure continued public access to them. They also take into account the contributions good buildings make as rich and satisfying environments for the discharge of the business of living. They take into account, too, that as attributes of fixed and durable buildings, the lessons of architectural expression persist in particular places and give those places their identities—local identities that

The twentieth-century American identity!

Morning in Grand Central Terminal: the impact of arrival at the nation's place of self-fulfillment

Robert Venturi's Guild House in Philadelphia: readable architectural expression

in turn help individuals and societies in turn organize their personal identities.

Laws seeking to protect the meanings of architecture engage it at its most interesting and rewarding edge, where the designing mind puts together for each building its expressive identity. That identity is the meaning offered by the building to any interested observer taking in the various impacts of its form and ornamentation and integrating them into an understanding of the proposal the building as a whole makes to the observer's intelligence. The impacts of form are what the observer generally first takes in directly and intuitively, feeling immediately good about a curve or troubled by a mass or an angle or walking into a great space and saying " . . . !" The impacts of ornament are all the myriad other effects of shape and detail the observer takes in by a more reflective and cerebral act of reading, making out the significance of a sign that says "Guild House" or an assembly of stone curls and leaves associated with the virtues of ancient Rome or of a roof having the coziness of Queen Anne. The elements of expression work seamlessly together; ornament is also felt as form and form is read as ornament. They are bound together in the relationships and order set by the hierarchy of the composition, the internal system of relative importance that controls its outcome as expression. That complete and integrated expressive outcome is meaning, as when we realize that Jefferson's Lawn at the University of Virginia is a proposal about the aspirations of the early republic or that the Kansai airport is a proposal about the diminution of the globe.

Laws protecting the expressive identities of buildings require understanding what those identities are and how they change. Understanding what they are is a matter of appreciation, the work of devoted observers to make out the expressive proposals of particular buildings and classify them by relative

The University of Virginia:
the heavens respond to Thomas
Jefferson's architectural device
for enlightment

The arc of Renzo Piano's Kansai
International Airport cuts in the
earth the smaller globe of aviation

Gerrit Rietveld's Schroeder House in Utrecht abstracts and restates the ideas of its row

worth, having in mind what the public ought to try to keep in order to protect its possibility of understanding itself. Understanding how identities change starts with an acknowledgment that because buildings serve in the real world, they inevitably acquire or become involved in new and different proposals of meaning all the time. Protecting their expression requires a capacity to appreciate the interaction of the successive proposals buildings inevitably make about themselves and about each other over time—the impacts of architecture on architecture—and to make principled judgments about the way they should change in light of the public's enduring need to have access to particular protected meanings. The judgments must be principled, not just expressions of likes and dislikes, so that they can be arguable, predictable, and otherwise entitled to the force of law.

The impacts of architecture on architecture, to be understood and managed in the course of protection, are apparent in the process that creates what might collectively be called combined works. In works of this type, new architecture is added to old architecture to meet some need for change, creating a new combined identity expressing new meanings. Combined works arise deliberately as a particular building is adapted to meet evolving needs, or involuntarily as it acquires a new neighbor, or finds itself in a changed neighborhood. However they arise, they represent in the best instances the work of successive intelligences taking advantage of and adding to existing expressive material and generating in the process valuable new combined meanings. In each case their success is a function of value received, value added, and value generated by the interaction of the two.

The evolution of meaning in successful combined works is vividly illustrated in architectural masterpieces that are themselves combinations of masterworks. The three considered in chapter 1—Saint Peter's Church, the Queen's House and the Greenwich Royal Naval Hospital, and the Castelvecchio—help define the class and set standards for its best possibilities. They offer satisfying paradigms for successful work with important existing architecture as a matter both of the design process and of the principles that give the process rigor. In so doing they suggest a rational basis for the judgments essential to the management of change in protected architecture.

The basis for judgment suggested by the paradigms is borne out in chapter 2 in a consideration of twentieth-century combined works that come to grips with modernism, the century's most important and provocative architectural initiative. Modernism vastly extended the expressive reach of architects and stretched the apparent expressive distance between their works and the works of their predecessors. The sample of works discussed illustrates the way modernism enriched the expressive range of combined works and reaffirmed at the same time the measure for success and the process and principles likely to produce it. The sample also confirms another suggestion of the paradigms, that there are no inherent or categorical limitations on the kinds of expression that can successfully be put together. Success is always a matter of the way it is done.

The basis for judgment suggested by the paradigms and by this body of combined work is then applied in chapter 3 to a sample of twentieth-century preservation cases as a principle by which to organize and measure the success of contemporary efforts to manage the impacts of new architecture on publicly valued buildings, particularly those protected by law. In these cases general

appreciation of impact becomes a specific obligation to understand a particular protected expressive identity and the impact on it of a proposed design. The judgment involves not just seeing the way the protected expression is accommodated in the combined work but enforcing a certain level of recognition of the protected identity in the combined work, ensuring that it enjoys in the combined expression the position to which it is entitled because of its acknowledged public worth.

A number of very recent combinations are then reviewed in chapter 4, returning from preservation to the larger question of combined works as a design paradigm. These offer an opportunity to reflect on the impacts on old buildings of current preoccupations of architects and to savor some of the rewards of the collaboration of old and new in the contemporary architecture of additions.

Alexander Hamilton's Manhattan farm squeezed by an apartment building and a church: a crude impact of architecture on architecture

*1-1. The Queen's House
and the Greenwich Royal
Naval Hospital*

1 The Evolution of Expression in Combined Works: Lessons from the Masters

Each creative act involves an exchange. Each new work of art is supported and enriched by its sources and its cultural and physical contexts. Once in existence, the new work in turn revises its sources and contexts, acting on them directly or requiring that they be reevaluated in light of its presence. The appreciation of a new work of art thus involves understanding its particular meaning as well as the traditions and forms that give value to its novelty and which its novelty changes and enriches. In each creative act the old and the new are inextricably entwined and inescapably beholden to each other.

The interaction of old and new in works of art is particularly evident in architecture. New buildings restate the meanings of old ones all the time (fig. 1-1), sometimes by replacing them, sometimes by reworking them to add or subtract expressive material. In the commonest cases, additions stand beside predecessor buildings. Sometimes they stand on top of them, as was proposed at Grand Central. They renew the meaning of old design work directly and deliberately or simply by association, as Sir Norman Foster's neighboring Law Faculty does in its obvious goodwill toward James Stirling's History Faculty Library at Cambridge University (discussed in chapter 4). New and old buildings work on each other from the start and continue to work on each other quietly over long periods of time, as, for example, Gropius's Harkness Quadrangle at Harvard University looks better every day when understood against forty subsequent years of architectural experiment (fig. 1-2).

The interactions of architecture are particularly interesting in combined works, where old and new designs are put together deliberately so that they will be understood together and judged for what they do to each other and in combination. Here the old and the new may have widely differing roles. The old may be saved as background

1-2. The Bauhaus modernism of Walter Gropius's Harkness Quadrangle at Harvard seems clean and unpretentious

Note: The darkest portions of the site plan diagrams are the oldest.

Not all buildings in each sequence are shown. The dates are approximate dates of final completion of each architect's contribution.

Up is not necessarily north.

SAINT PETER'S CHURCH
Rome, Italy

Donato Bramante, 1506
Michelangelo Buonarotti, 1564
Carlo Maderno, 1612
Gian Lorenzo Bernini, 1667

1-3. Michelangelo's tremendous dome for Saint Peter's marks the pole of the Roman Catholic globe

1-4. From Serlio, the simple round church plan implied under the dome

1-5. Bramante's elegant airy Renaissance vessel for a readily accessible relic

1-6. Michelangelo's much more monumental container with only one official way in to the tomb

1-7. Maderno's nave adds an awesome obligatory approach

to the new or may clearly be brought out as the object celebrated in the combined work of art. In these combinations the participating works illuminate each other, bring out each other's value, and, ideally, create new values in the combination well beyond the value of the parts.

Three architectural masterworks—Saint Peter's, the Queen's House and the Greenwich Royal Naval Hospital, and the Castelvecchio—vividly, and quite differently, illustrate the finest possibilities for combined works of this kind.

SAINT PETER'S CHURCH

The architectural history of new Saint Peter's, Rome, represents the most ordinary form of architectural evolution by addition, elevated to the highest level by a matchless succession of late Renaissance and baroque masters. These architects fitted the growing building to the evolving response of the Roman Catholic church to the Protestant Reformation in the process, celebrating, changing, and reusing Michelangelo's magnificent dome (fig. 1-3).

The similar schemes of two masters, Bramante and Michelangelo, start the sequence and show in their differences the direction it will take. In both schemes the building plan and its dome are centered on the crucial single point, the physical and spiritual destination of the church program, the tomb of Saint Peter. In plan the tomb is the center of the circle of a Serlian round church implied by the dome (fig. 1-4) and the intersection of the axes of the square plans laid by both schemes on top of the underlying circle in the plans for the dome's actual base. In section the tomb is the object of the single vertical axis of the powerful, tall dome. The dome holds up the same vertical axis in the outside world, wrapped in the round temple of its lantern to mark the physical and spiritual pole of its church.

1-3

In Bramante's scheme (fig. 1-5) the spiritual destination, surrounded by an elegant, porous poché, would have been celebrated in a building that held it out for general veneration like a giant Renaissance reliquary. The tomb would have been immediately accessible through at least four equal doors from all directions of the globe, the center of a humanist diagram for the place of divinity and its church in the world. In Michelangelo's design for the actual building, the diagram changes substantially (fig. 1-6). The dome now calls attention to the crucial point as an event in the world, but the poché around it is much heavier and the container correspondingly more monumental, the church less open to the world and more something to get into if the destination is to be reached.

To get in, all directions are no longer equally favored. Instead, one side of the building is extended and much emphasized by a great portico marking the single official way in and, at the same time, the beginning of an important architectural retreat from the tomb.

Maderno continues this evolution when he stretches Michelangelo's portico into the great nave that organizes veneration within the building (fig. 1-7). The dome and its destination are now viewed at a distance and approached only in a specified procession over a significant distance in awesome architectural circumstances. At the beginning of the procession, Maderno's new façade (fig. 1-8) partially obscures Michelangelo's dome, reducing its role and making the destination accessible only after certain lessons have been absorbed. These lessons are not the engaging fables of Romanesque and Gothic porches but rather a single majestic display of classical order. The façade is now penetrated less on the basis of the general invitation extended by the dome than in response to a particular command.

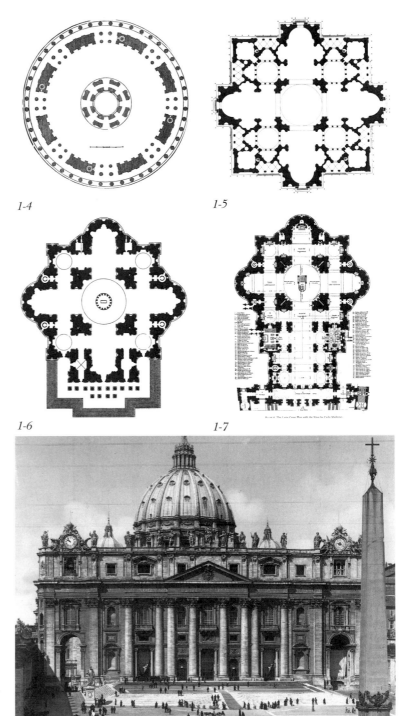

1-4

1-5

1-6

1-7

1-8

1-8. Maderno's facade puts its command in front of the dome

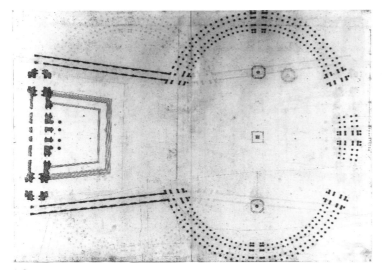

1-9

1-10

1-9. Bernini's double ellipse collects the faithful and ties them into the axis of the procession

1-10. The portico enclosure wraps all the way around and holds them in place

Bernini continues the architectural extension away from the tomb with his extraordinary portico and colonnade (fig. 1-9). The arms of the colonnade begin by literally falling back from the façade and drawing in toward the center so that, at the plane of the colonnade's focus, the dome is once again fully revealed centered over and behind the façade, but at a new and greater distance. The two curved colonnades open out to hold a space that Bernini carefully makes an ellipse, not another circle, so that it will have an axis of its own and lock in at the bottom of the geometrical sequence that leads up to the climactic single point in the circle under the dome. The columns are aligned to focus into the ellipse so that it acts as a porous, accessible collector and organizer for those gathering from the surrounding open space (fig. 1-10). The columns thus reestablish some of the same inviting porosity of Bramante's plan, but at a distance from the tomb, at the beginning of the now much longer official sequence toward it and under the control of its powerful architecture. With the axis of the ellipse addressing the façade and intersecting the axis of the prescribed procession to the tomb, the forced perspective of the colonnade drives the crowd toward the façade and through the sequence to the spiritual destination under the dome. There the huge upward-waving columns of Bernini's wonderful baldachin dramatize to the now quite distant faithful its offer of vertical motion out of this world.

Bernini adds his colonnade to extend and rebalance the entire composition, reintegrating Michelangelo's dome into the great architectural engine that organizes and delivers the climax of the spiritual journey. The beneficiary is a crowd much evolved from Bramante's, operating under very different rules of engagement with its divinity by way of the church of the Counter-Reformation. At the same time it stresses

20

Maderno's façade as a controlling intermediary between the faithful and the tomb, arranging and holding its crowds at distances and within sightlines that impose on them the full benefit of the whole composition (fig. 1-11), including the annual blessing delivered by the Pope at Easter from one of Maderno's windows.

The success of the evolution completed by Bernini is illuminated by contrast in the work of the last "architect" significantly to try to update it, Benito Mussolini. His contribution comes when in the 1930s he skewers the composition on the straight axis of the Via della Conciliazione. While Bernini's terzo braccio—the final pavilion that would have completed the ellipse—was never built, his container remained finite, extended not unmanageably by the closed rectangular space of the Piazza Rusticucci. By blowing out the bottom of the enclosure to make the Via della Conciliazione, Mussolini does what he can to demote Bernini's collector to an incident in a forced march of obelisks, and the church and its dome to common landmarks in the banal drama of the Fascist City (fig. 1-12).

THE QUEEN'S HOUSE AND THE GREENWICH ROYAL NAVAL HOSPITAL

Christopher Wren's integration of Inigo Jones's house for Queen Anne in the Greenwich Royal Naval Hospital is very different from the growth of Saint Peter's as a vessel for a single evolving purpose. The Hospital is instead an unexpected composition of very different parts made to work together under duress, an admirable preservation case where an imposed public constraint—in this case the command of Queen Mary—brings out the best in a master.

Jones's Queen's House was built as gatehouse and hunting pavilion for a royal park in 1635. When Wren addressed the villa

1-11

1-12

1-11. Aerial view of Saint Peter's: the cumulative effect of all the additions

1-12. Mussolini's fascist parade to a landmark Saint Peter's

**THE QUEEN'S HOUSE AND
THE GREENWICH ROYAL
NAVAL HOSPITAL**

Greenwich, England

Inigo Jones, 1635
John Webb, 1667
Christopher Wren, 1715

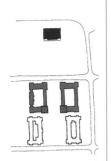

1-13. Queen Anne's Palladian country house at Greenwich, by Inigo Jones

1-14. Jones's original sketch for the Queen's House as a hunting pavilion straddling the road and giving access to the royal park

nearly a century later, it still enjoyed great royal favor and, possibly, general recognition as a pioneering landmark of English Palladianism (fig. 1-13). The ingenious way the original design (fig. 1-14) accommodated a public road running through the ground floor and provided a means to get over the adjacent enclosure wall had been lost to intervening changes. On the other hand, the revolutionary clarity and simplicity of its form—Jones's version of the seminal lumps of building by which Andrea Palladio marked the place of Renaissance humans in the universe of the Veneto—was still apparent and it was still important as the controlling object of a picturesque landscape composition on the slope up from the Thames to the Tudor palace that became the Greenwich Observatory.

It may never have occurred to Wren to try to incorporate the Queen's House in a composition from which it was physically remote and that had, as a tribute of a kind to national maritime power, very different expressive objectives. His first scheme established a long court with its axis up from the river aligned with the House, but this court was closed short of the House with a dome (fig. 1-15). Though views of this scheme look at it from the river, Wren may have seen the dome at the head of his composition as not a bad complement to the House when looked at from the other direction. In any event, the Queen's House would not have been part of the composition and would have been cut off from the river and much reduced in importance in the landscape (fig. 1-16).

The relationship of the Queen's House to the river was important to Queen Mary, who rejected Wren's scheme and set him a serious compositional challenge. The center and top of the hierarchy of his new composition now had to be kept open so that it could be filled at a distance by Jones's Queen's House (fig. 1-17). To meet the chal-

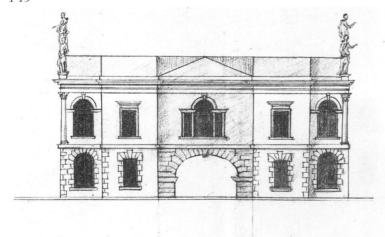

1-14

1-15. Christopher Wren's first design for a monumental hospital ignores the Queen's House

1-16. Wren's proposed elevation builds up to its own climactic dome

1-17. Wren's second elevation uses two domes to make the Queen's House the climax of the composition

1-15

1-16

1-17

1-18. *The knuckles of Wren's plan become sharper and the domes grow taller*

1-19. *The Hospital swings the Queen's House into view at the end of its axis.*

1-20. *Honored by Wren and his successors, the Queen's House controls an unusual naval monument.*

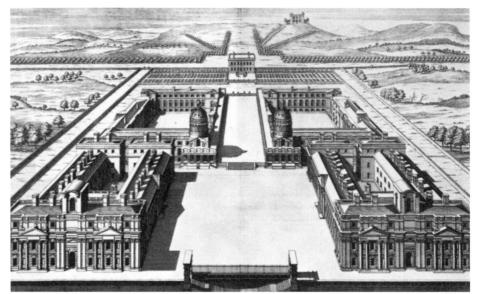

1-18

1-19

1-20

lenge, Wren drew the two parallel pavilions nearest to the House closer together, as if to fit it better. Drawing them in, he exposed their corners and made them sites for domed towers marking the ends of the two principal compositional elements of the new Hospital—the chapel and the banquet hall—and bracketing the court leading to the House. These towers and the elements they control grew in prominence and interest as the design matured (fig. 1-18). Because there are two of them, however, they always balance each other and never replace the House as the single center of the composition. In their final state the two remarkable towers simultaneously give the Hospital its own powerful presence and guarantee its subordination to the House.

The lift the Queen's House gets from the slope of the site strengthens it for its role at the top of the hierarchy. This emphasis is reinforced by the attention the House is paid by other elements of Wren's dynamic composition. The towers, round at the top and square at the bottom, frame the House and provide a pivot for the movement of the colonnades that tie the composition together at a level well below the cornice of the Queen's House. The vertical development of the towers redivides the heights of the chapel and banquet hall so that they in turn tie into the composition at the height of the colonnades. These start with relatively stable pairs of columns facing the river, turn sharply at the corners of the towers, and then resolve themselves into long, simple, continuous ranges that run up toward the House. The colonnades' rhythm of dark and light shifts from the greater reflectivity of the paired columns facing the river to the relatively uniform darkness of the final runs. These end at the single flat reflective surface of the House, the principal surface of its kind in the composition. At the head of the long axis the stable form of the House itself is animated by the composi-

tion; it moves quickly in and out of view depending on the viewer's relationship to the axis itself—an activity readily apparent from the river or the park across the river from it (fig. 1-19).

When in view, the plain white block of the House makes vivid the evolution from Jones's simple humanist forms to Wren's athletic, baroque celebration of power (fig. 1-20). Wren was prepared to go further to integrate the House into the Hospital, with ranks of hospital wards filling in the distance between the two. Interesting as this might have been, it might have upset the balance of the present composition. As it is, the House benefits from and contributes to a setting that never could have been foreseen for it, receiving in the exchange a new formal stature as something other than a pleasure palace and the chance to participate in a new expression of royal authority. The House in turn raises the stakes for Wren, forcing from him a virtuoso tribute to the sacrifices of the King's military servants that simultaneously acknowledges an allegiance to royal qualities of a very different character maintained in the place of honor.

THE CASTELVECCHIO

Carlo Scarpa's 1960s transformation of the Castelvecchio in Verona (fig. 1-21) is a masterwork of combined architecture made in a context different from Saint Peter's or the Greenwich Hospital. It brings home the extraordinary power of the possibilities opened for twentieth-century architects by the modernist embrace of abstraction and the opportunity they acquired to develop new meanings for buildings where old meanings had been cut away. In Scarpa's case the abstraction is literally a cutting away to reveal new meanings for the della Scala family castle and to expose and use them in the service of its contemporary life as a museum.

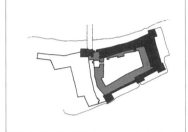

1-21

1-22

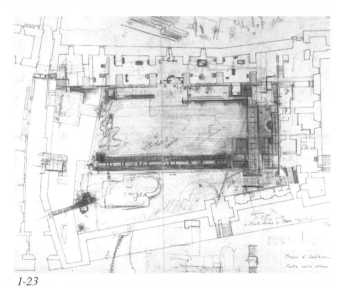

1-23

1-21. *The della Scala family fortress on the Adige River in Verona*

1-22. *The unchanged street face of the fortress*

1-23. *Carlo Scarpa's plan for internal change*

1-24. *Scarpa's bronze and concrete introduction to the issues in the fortress*

1-25. *Strong walls and strong rooms hold the Castelvecchio's treasures*

1-24

1-25

In the renewed museum, nothing obvious is added onto the body of the castle (fig. 1-22), as Scarpa instead mines it, in both the geologic and the military senses, for space and meaning (fig. 1-23). He addresses the building from the first as a castle, as a body of resistance, a container of value associated with life and death, to be subdued in a demonstration of the power of the art that is its new master. At the front door his concrete entry extrusion introduces the issues of mass, strength, and enclosure dealt with by his art and pulls visitors inside with its hook (fig. 1-24). Inside, he carves out within the great folded length of the fortress a rhythmical sequence of vaulted strongholds of space and light (fig. 1-25) guarded by gates (fig. 1-26) presenting and protecting the museum's truly precious objects.

1-26

Within these rooms Scarpa's reveals include gaps at the edges of the new floors showing off the enclosing masonry and beautifully framed holes showing treasures below the floor. The tight, staggered steps cut into the fortress wall force attention, step by labored step, to the mass, bearing, and literal resistance of the ramparts to which they give access (fig. 1-27). Other, larger carvings away call attention to the same issues, like the jagged cut down through the full height of the river wall at its junction with an adjacent tower (fig. 1-28). The sharp, down-driving cut shows off the dramatic height of the wall, the sensuous uniformity of its surface, and the huge latent energy of resistance in its great mass.

At the top of the hierarchy of all the reveals, finally, is the one Scarpa makes the climax of the experience of the museum, the titanic reveal that focuses on the Can Grande statue (fig. 1-29). Displaying the innards of the walls, the structure, and the roof in a kind of exploded diagram, this reveal seems torn from the castle in a show of architectural power amounting to violence, as if only a bomb could subdue the

1-27

1-28

1-26. Inside the treasury, Scarpa opens a window down into the foundation

1-27. A Scarpa stair crosses from new to old and up the resistant rampart

1-28. The slash by the tower dramatizes the height and power of the wall

1-29

1-29. The great gap blown for Can Grande della Scala

1-30. Can Grande in his original setting

1-31. Can Grande, warrior of immortality

immense resistance of the old fortress and allow its new master to capture its value as a museum for the protection of art. Like all his other interventions, the resulting rent is beautifully composed and detailed, a satisfying triumph not of brutality but of design.

Scarpa makes obvious the old fortress's service of this new master in the focus of his great rent on the funerary monument of its old master, Can Grande della Scala (fig. 1-30), founder of the castle and patron of Verona's arts. Scarpa makes the funerary statue of Verona's own condottiere the culmination of the hierarchy he forces on the fortress and, in the intensity of its own connection as art with war, struggle, and death, the point of reference he offers for his understanding of the fortress's meaning as a museum. To help the aggressive little statue succeed in its role, Scarpa raises it up to the second floor so that it stands in the middle of the linear itinerary of the museum (fig. 1-31). He turns it to direct its inherent energy back into the composition and into the museum and sets it in the middle of the great rent blown by his architecture in the old instrument of war, bringing home in the size of the rent the power of the issues embodied in the statue. With the resistance of the fortress blown back around him, the representative of all the art in the Castelvecchio—its armed, male Mona Lisa—is pleased to pause for us on Scarpa's jutting bracket in his unending tilt with death.

Maderno, Bernini, Wren, and Scarpa all worked with existing buildings designed by remarkable predecessors, drawing the structures out and giving them changed meaning as contributing parts of new combined works of art, demonstrating in the process a highly successful approach to design with old buildings. Willing or no, each of these masters was committed to the existing building as a source of value to be explored, understood, and developed. By virtue of this commit-

1-30

1-31

ment, the old works came not just to participate in but also to control the outcome.
Thus to a substantial extent Michelangelo
set the terms for Bernini, as Jones did for
Wren and as the author of the Castelvecchio
did for Scarpa. In each case the resulting
combined work became a collaboration.

The result of the collaboration is not just
a general sense of comfort and happiness in
the relationship worked out between the
old and the new but a particular satisfaction
at the places the new and the old take in the
combined work. The values of the old
engaged in the new design work wind up at

or near the head of its hierarchy. Bernini
helps restore the dome of Saint Peter's to its
place as the ultimate representative of the
spiritual destination of the Church of Rome.
Wren transforms the Queen's House from a
pleasure pavilion loose in a landscape to the
focus of a large and active commemoration
of national duty and power. Scarpa cuts out
of the ancient Castelvecchio a forceful
demonstration of the issues in its art's pursuit of immortality. In each case the new
work celebrates the old and secures it an
appropriate place in the service of the
meaning of the combination.

2-1. Gustave Eiffel introduces a startling new order of architectural expression in Paris

2 Twentieth-Century Combined Works: The Expressive Possibilities of Modernism

S aint Peter's, the Greenwich Royal Naval Hospital, and the Castelvecchio set a very high standard for successful combinations of new and old architecture. An understanding of combined works beyond such obvious paradigms requires a broader view of the range of successful combinations possible in the twentieth century.

The controversial addition to the City of Paris of the great, strange form of the Eiffel tower (fig. 2-1) can mark the start of the proliferation of expressive possibilities that accelerated in the twentieth century with the establishment of modernist attitudes to ornament and their celebration of function as the central business of architectural expression. The Eiffel Tower made vivid the expressive potential of new forms generated by evolving building technology—notably, the leaps of scale and shape technology made possible to serve new orders of human demand. The modernists' embrace of these possibilities, and their purge of conventional architectural ornament, restarted a pursuit of devices to express a gradually widening and heterodox celebration of what buildings do in the service of human demand and, more broadly, what they are about.

With modernism, architecture, like every other art in the century, embraced abstraction and its implications for the development of expression. With the help of abstraction, oppressive conventions about the expression of buildings were disassembled, the exposed parts redeveloped in accordance with newly apparent rules and then reassembled to celebrate in new ways an ethical core of meanings the conventions had come to obscure. Thus in the 1960s, in reaction to a modernism that had itself become conventional, Robert Venturi, a distinguished writer, could abstract, rethink, and restore readable ornament as a component of architectural expression. The ingenious and poetic *homo faber* Renzo Piano could disassemble, recombine, and hold up

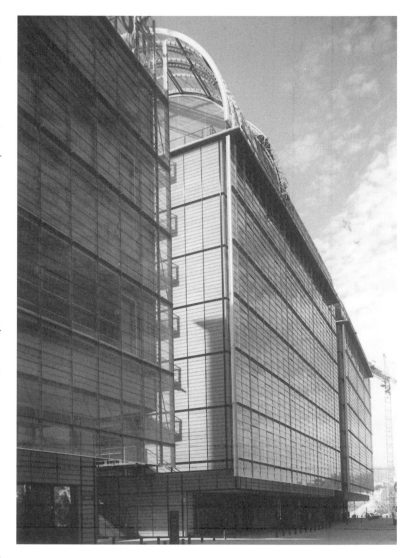

2-2. Renzo Piano shows off the exterior wall as complex instrument of enclosure at the Cité Internationale in Lyon

for contemplation the building envelope as a complex and beautiful instrument of human service (fig. 2-2). The resulting proliferation of possibilities stretched what had before been a relatively comfortable evolution of meaning from work to work, obliging it to accommodate substantial, even violent, expressive incongruities. For the interested observer of architecture, asked to leave the comfort of conventions that served architecture the way realism served painting or tonality served music, the resolution of these incongruities into new understandings of meaning required an important new effort.

The works in this chapter illustrate a range of successful combinations that reward the effort to understand the impacts on old buildings of a variety of twentieth-century expressive agendas. The examples are grouped loosely by the ways in which their expressions go together: where the new extends meanings of the old, where the new derives new meanings from the old, and where the new intentionally transforms the meaning of old. The examples illustrate the manifold results of the pursuit by important architects of different expressive agendas, working with the devices they prefer and within the limits of their particular gifts as designers. The examples suggest that when works are successful, even across vast differences in expressive possibility, their architects have understood the meaning of the original building, used it to illuminate their work and their work to illuminate it, and combined the new and the old in the service of a common goal. Both new and old play a role in the hierarchy of the combined work that appropriately contributes to the new combined meaning.

Extension

The simplest combined works are extensions of old buildings in wings or similar attachments. Additions of this kind set out to do new parts of an old business with relative independence, each following its own expressive agenda. When the original building and the extension are seen together, the expressions may seem far apart. In successful instances, however, what emerges is an enriched set of insights about the purposes the old and the new both serve. The extension relies on the old as the ground for its novelty, extending the understanding of the old and making with it a greater and more important combined statement about their common business.

GÖTEBORG LAW COURTS

Gunnar Asplund's courthouse in Göteborg, Sweden (fig. 2-3), is a remarkable demonstration of the way the resources of twentieth-century architecture—here an abstraction that seems purifying and refreshing—enlarged architects' expressive possibilities and allowed them to extend old buildings in combinations that would again properly represent activities that had themselves significantly evolved.

Asplund worked on the courthouse from the time he entered the competition for the job, which he won in 1913, until the building was completed in 1937. In that twenty-four-year period he prepared a fascinating succession of schemes that illustrate the evolving convictions of a master at work. In the end, his collaboration with the fine old building bore fruit at just the right time in his career.

The strongly axial neoromantic scheme that won the competition (fig. 2-4) would have demolished Nicodemus Tessin's 1670s courthouse, turning its entry away from the adjacent Gustaf Adolf Square. Asked to keep the old courthouse or at least to protect its relationship to the square, Asplund wrestled with intermediate approaches concerning the entry (fig. 2-5) and internal circulation

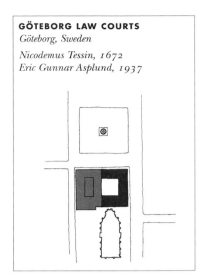

GÖTEBORG LAW COURTS
Göteborg, Sweden

Nicodemus Tessin, 1672
Eric Gunnar Asplund, 1937

2-3. Nicodemus Tessin's Göteborg
Courthouse with Gunnar Asplund's
addition

2-4. Asplund's winning neoromantic
scheme of 1913 would have changed
everything

2-3

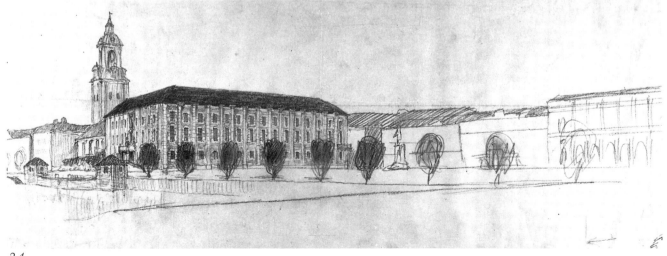

2-4

2-5

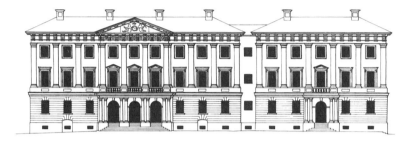

2-6

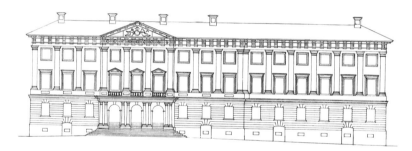

2-7

2-5. *Asplund begins to classicize the scheme*

2-6. *The old building restored, with a derivative annex design*

2-7. *The annex pushed out like an extrusion*

and sketched elevations that emulated or preserved the original façade. He tried out a variety of conventional expressions for the building, particularly in the early 1920s, when the project seems to have come close to construction (fig. 2-6).

The extraordinary resolution came in the 1930s. By then, Asplund was a confirmed modernist who had completed the Stockholm Library and the rigorously modern Stockholm Exposition. When he picked up the courthouse design again in 1934, he nevertheless proposed versions of the derivative façades of his 1920s schemes, simplifying them into a kind of official Washington, D.C.–Pennsylvania Avenue extruded classicism (fig. 2-7). Possibly Asplund was not sure what do with his modernism when faced again with the old building or felt the discipline of modernism required a clear separation of the old, with its constraints, and the new, with its possibilities. Or he was willing to lapse into a conventional respect for the old building to reassure its sponsors.

Then he tried out modern schemes, offering a very plain modern extension to replace the Pennsylvania Avenue extrusion (fig. 2-8). He then made a series of changes to enrich the relationship of the annex to the old building. He clarified the joint between the old and the new so that the new read as a comparable but dependent box. He rebalanced the solids and voids of the façade in favor of the solids, bringing it closer to the balance of the masonry original. He varied the sizes of the windows and added ornamental panels to call out the piano nobile and clarify the hierarchy of his façade, at the same time squaring the windows to make them work better with the new frame and differentiating them from the old windows by dividing them with a horizontal bar. The scheme was approved and construction began. During construction, Asplund made his last major design move, sliding the windows of the new façade off-center toward the old building. The move seemed to lock the annex into place, as if it had been inevitable all along (fig. 2-9).

The result is a milestone in the evolution of a master. The young Asplund would have taken the courthouse down. The modernist Asplund still hesitated to work with it, seeming to suggest that modernism could not be mixed with old buildings. But the mature Asplund took up the collaboration, to the benefit of the courthouse and also to his own, to the extent that work on the courthouse may have helped his progress toward the tempered severity of his great final work at the Woodland Crematorium.

The Courthouse, as a combined work, now offers a much enriched representation of Swedish attitudes to criminal justice, its intended mixture of formality, openness, and rationality (fig. 2-10). Next to the old courthouse, the annex is a box of courtrooms and offices comparable to the original but flatter, plainer, and more utilitarian, as if pulled out of the original to make the actual contents of the formal old container obvious and accessible. This sense of exposure is emphasized by the thin panels of the annex enclosure, which look a little like the back side of the inside. On the surface of the box, the structure of the annex is shown as a strongly expressed frame, as if exposed to emphasize the rational structure that underpins symbolic façades like the old one and ideally underpins the whole judicial enterprise. The exposed frame reads as a grid, an abstract tool for rational organization and an emblem of the rationality and order sought inside.

The combined façade's mixed representation of formality and reason perfectly introduces what is going on inside. The approach to justice invokes the authority of the original façade—this is still the same, serious business. The entry sequence moves up the old steps and through the open arches in the base of the old building. Inside it

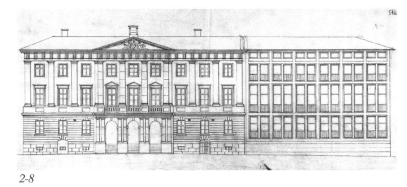

2-8

2-9

2-10

2-8. *The big turn of events in 1934: Asplund tries out possibilities of abstraction*

2-9. *The final design locked in place by its asymmetric windows*

2-10. *The addition as built*

2-11. The courtyard at the juncture of old and new

2-12. Asplund's long, contemplative stair

2-13. The blank walls of John Trumbull's original windowless gallery at Yale in 1832

2-11

2-12

2-13

turns in a carefully landscaped and ornamented open court and enters the annex (fig. 2-11), where the public business is now actually done. There Asplund's exquisite, airy top-lit interior court with its graceful, impossible-to-hurry stair (fig. 2-12) and delicate wood details and furnishings invites reflection and discussion before any formal proceeding. It in turn gives access to courtrooms flooded with light, where lay justices at low wooden benches seem ready to judge but equally eager to talk things out. As a prosecutor observed, "If you have to prosecute, it's a good place to do it!"

While the annex was highly controversial at first, the combined work now seems quietly self-assured. The expressive differences of the old and new are muted by the pale yellow the buildings share and by what seems now an obvious recall in the exposed annex frame of the plain white pilasters common in traditional Swedish architecture. The hierarchy of the whole is beautifully balanced with the symbolic building still foremost, the supporting annex using its modern difference not just to assert its relative plainness and subordination but also to say something important about the work within the courthouse as a whole. Formality, rationality, and openness—even friendliness—are integrated in an enviable representation of what justice should be.

YALE UNIVERSITY ART GALLERY

Louis I. Kahn's 1953 Yale Art Gallery addition in New Haven, Connecticut, is an important early display of the simplicity, power, and strangeness of his mature work. The addition is the tail of a long historic sequence of gallery buildings that began with Yale's original Trumbull Gallery in 1832, a building once described as a wedding of a mausoleum and a country house and long since demolished (fig. 2-13). Some of the Trumbull Gallery's character can still be appreciated in the architecture of Yale's several surviving secret society "tombs," notably that of Skull and Bones, from the same era, which survives around the corner. While Trumbull's windowless gallery may have connected with the German romanticism immortalized in the tombs, its greater purpose was to maximize wall space, provide light from above, and promote concentration. In an early American purpose-built art gallery, Trumbull addressed the same issues as Kahn and came up with a not dissimilar public display of the role of the wall.

The present sequence of art buildings starts with Yale's second, Street Hall, a small Gothic Revival pile surviving on the corner of Yale's Old Campus (fig. 2-14). Egerton Swartwout's powerful Collegiate Gothic bridge gallery attaches to Street Hall and carries the sequence across Wall Street to a big square corner tower (fig. 2-15) and then along the street to the sculpture gallery, a rectangular box with four large round-headed windows. The flat arch of the big bridge, the small round-headed windows of the tower, and the procession of strong, rhythmical, round-headed windows of the sculpture gallery animate an unusual, strong, linear composition.

Kahn's addition to the composition starts with a wide reveal just deep enough for the new entry to the added gallery, the next box in the sequence. The Art Gallery's entry is marked with a grander, abstracted version of the recess that opens the sculpture gallery. At the back of the reveal the unadorned brick of the attachment introduces the notion of the pure, smooth wall developed in the south wall that begins at the edge of the reveal (fig. 2-16). Set in the reveal, Kahn's entry turns toward the sequence of old galleries as if to acknowledge its energy and offer pedestrians a way to slip out of its stream. At the same time the reveal exposes and calls attention to the edge of the gallery's most important public feature, the nearly autonomous striped rectangular brick south wall (fig. 2-17).

YALE UNIVERSITY ART GALLERY
New Haven, Connecticut

John Trumbull, 1832
P. B. Wight, 1864
Egerton Swartwout, 1928
Louis I. Kahn, 1953

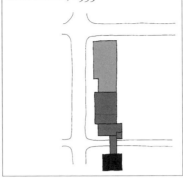

2-14. P. B. Wight's Street Hall in 1864 starts the present sequence

2-15. Egerton Swartwout's 1928 arches pick up from Street Hall, cross the street, and move west

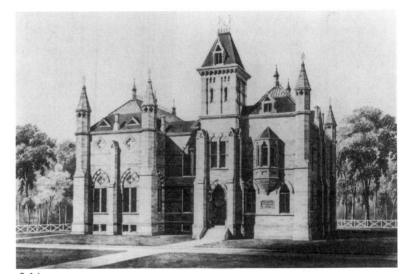

2-14

2-15

2-16

2-17

2-16. Louis I. Kahn abstracts
the idea in the next addition

2-17. At the entry Kahn's introductory wall displays the sequence
abstracted to infinity

Like all the abstracted elements by which Kahn introduces the meanings of his great buildings, the south wall is central to understanding Kahn's contribution. The length of the wall is tuned by the length of the reveal to give its rectangle the same proportions as its neighbor's, continuing the apparent march of block forms down the street. The wall fits the box exactly, defining the gallery as a container. The four stripes on the wall, which mark the edges of the floor slabs behind it, pick up and pass on the movement and energy of the window arches of the sculpture gallery, and of the whole sequence of gallery buildings, as if to infinity.

Showing off the south wall this way, Kahn also introduces the very different art gallery inside. This gallery is not a hall with great windows like its neighbor but a rectangular, horizontal, open slab of space in which art can be placed in infinite combinations. The space made by Kahn's famous tetrahedral concrete truss is glazed on all exterior sides except the south. There the south wall stands by itself, holding the building in place, organizing its entry, and isolating the gallery space from the street and the sun. In so doing it represents the new gallery like a sign, introducing it as a box and demonstrating the role of walls in art galleries: defining space, controlling light, guiding circulation, and holding up art. In the last it reflects the special interest of its curatorial era in holding up art in specific ways and combinations that require the viewer to meet the hung work in a controlled way. Such a gallery wall ideally has considerable locational freedom apart from its role as structure or enclosure so that it can be placed to generate a particular point of view, the way the pogo panels devised for Kahn's gallery can spring into place virtually anywhere between the gallery floors and the truss above (fig. 2-18). Likewise, Kahn's south wall seems itself to have been "placed" as the device to announce and manage the encounter of the public with the gallery, displaying in its stripes the abstracted essence of the architecture it extends.

The south wall thus enlarges the discussion of the architecture of the sequence of Yale art buildings with a display of the issues of its time. Taking a modern view of light control—in contrast to the great windows set up to fill its neighbor's interior volume with light—it dramatizes the possibility of excluding light altogether where appropriate. By showing its edge, it makes clear the difference between the universal exhibition space it protects and the traditional volume enclosed by its neighbor. And by making a point of its blankness—the gallery wall as important for what it displays—it makes a happy connection back along the sequence of both buildings and time to the blank walls of Trumbull's original mausoleum.

Kahn's gallery is no longer the end of the sequence of Yale art buildings. This now extends directly across the next street, where its energy is finally wrapped up and absorbed in the complexities of Paul Rudolph's muscular and demanding Art and Architecture building (fig. 2-19). Across the street, somehow not quite in the series, is Kahn's later Center for British Art. In its intermediate position in the series the Yale Art Gallery firmly, intelligently, and quite serenely maintains Kahn's contribution to the understandings of his predecessors and successors and to the evolving history of the art museum itself.

ALLEN MEMORIAL ART MUSEUM

Venturi and Rauch's 1977 Ellen Johnson Gallery in Oberlin, Ohio, is a startling attachment to an elegant, symmetrical Renaissance palazzo derived by Cass Gilbert from Brunelleschi in 1917 (fig. 2-20). Venturi and Rauch understood Gilbert's Allen Memorial Art Museum as a beautiful old building (fig. 2-21). They also felt they could not escape

2-18

2-19

2-18. A pogo panel displaying art

2-19. Paul Rudolph's Art and Architecture Building winds up the sequence in something more baroque

**ALLEN MEMORIAL
ART MUSEUM**
Oberlin, Ohio

Cass Gilbert, 1917
Venturi and Rauch, 1976

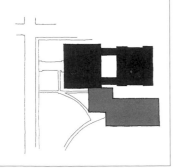

2-20

2-21

2-22

2-20. Cass Gilbert's Allen
Memorial Art Museum with
the Ellen Johnson Gallery of
Venturi and Rauch, Ober-
lin, Ohio

2-21. Gilbert's exposition of
the principles of high art

2-22. The inescapable low-
art neighbor

2-23. Venturi's design
engages both

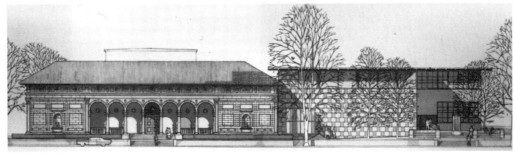

2-23

the complex and unusual attitude toward socially desirable construction expressed in its context. They seized the conflict between the old building and its context as an opportunity to test the worth of their own interest in ornament—in expressive elements that are "read" to appeal to the mind—as a source of devices to resolve it.

The Allen addresses a beautiful college green and is paired with a corner filling station (fig. 2-22), the inescapable American condition acknowledged and celebrated by Venturi in his writing and his work. Down the street, on the other side of the Allen, is a swoopy freestanding Wallace Harrison auditorium trumpeting its self-importance at the green. Beyond the auditorium a generic modern motel completes this scraggly all-American streetscape.

To address these complexities, Venturi and Rauch attach to the Allen asymmetrical plain boxes, or sheds (fig. 2-23), as Venturi put it in an article in the *Museum Bulletin*. They decorate the sheds to make them into a polemic about art and architecture notable for itself and the way it engages and expands the meaning of Gilbert's palazzo.

The argument begins with the placement of the addition, a small, square box gallery attached to the old building and a second, bigger rectangular box of studios and workrooms hung off the first in an L along the side of the symmetrical original. The placement was dictated in part by an addition that had already expanded the museum symmetrically to the rear. To the architects, the asymmetry was also a way of engaging the symmetry of the old as little as possible, so as not to destroy it. The asymmetry, however, immediately calls attention to the extension as something that attaches to but does not go with the original in an obvious way. The resolution of the two occurs only once the mind is engaged, when the observer reads the elements of the new expression as ornament like words on a page.

2-24. Venturi's decorated sheds elaborate the issues in Cass Gilbert's old canon of beauty

Set up to be read on the surfaces of the sheds, Venturi's elements are abstracted so that they make their connections not only literally by their sameness but also by reference to the issues they and Gilbert have in common (fig. 2-24). The two boxes of the addition read as volumes like Gilbert's building but outlined rather than solid. Their walls are thin like billboards, vehicles for messages rather than built solids like the walls of the original building. Gilbert's tiled hip roof, cornice, and elegant black-accented frieze become a flat projecting roof edge with a frieze of shadow and clerestory windows. His beautifully laid-up true masonry façade becomes a flat pattern of applied stone pieces in alternating colors on the skin of the addition. The composition of the new façade is anchored to Gilbert's by a single, flat, almost square window, the kind of opening associated with openings punched in masonry but now in a wall with no thickness to punch. A structural column clearly visible behind and in the middle of the window emphasizes the wall's importance as a bearer of meaning rather than of weight and the window's importance as a connector by reference rather than as a window. Next to it the actual connection occurs as a much-big-

2-25

2-25. *Gilbert, the sheds, and an example of the art they can accommodate together*

2-26. *The emblem of Venturi's good-natured reconciliation*

2-26

ger-than-need-be soft joint that makes as much of the idea as of the fact of connection and rubbing in the point of the polemic by making Gilbert's wall look just as paper-thin.

The elements enrich the combination by making multiple references. The abstracted shadow of the new overhang, for example, refers to Gilbert's overhang but also adds a connection to the shadows of the overhangs of the Prairie houses of Frank Lloyd Wright. In so doing it reminds us that Gilbert built Brunelleschi in America and specifically in the Middle West, where the same element has been made to serve other very different but equally valid expressive purposes. It points out, that is, that Gilbert's was only one of several expressive possibilities operable even in his time. At the same time they make possible a reconciliation of his architecture with an art he could hardly have anticipated (fig. 2-25). The elements making these connections by reference are all exaggerated so that their expression has an edge, an edge softened by the way their exaggeration makes them funny, like the giant soft joint or the jolly Ionic column often used as an emblem for the new museum (fig. 2-26). The exaggeration makes them obviously artifices and parts of a persistent argument, with a character that keeps the argument good-humored.

The final meaning of the argument turns on the way these elements set up and participate in the "hierarchies among ordinary and ideal elements, and plain and fancy styles" that Venturi finds organize Gilbert's aesthetic and that organize the new combined work. Thus the new sets up a progression with the old—from "fancy" to "plain," from concrete to abstract, from serious to funny, from the fanciest part of all, Gilbert's old palazzo, through the less decorated shed of the gallery connector to the very plain factory-like workshops—and on by implication to the filling station and the other complexities and contradictions of their common context.

That Gilbert's building should be the "fanciest" is finally the point of the argument. At the top of the hierarchy it is still the most contrived, still a complex expressive choice, not a separate truth, properly linked by the argument of Venturi's addition to the very different choices around it. As the fanciest, however, it is also the most complete, integrated, and resolved, with every piece by its rules beautifully in place. At the top of the hierarchy of a teaching museum, Gilbert's "beautiful old building" is shown off in all its own instructive artifice as a complete, built canon of beauty.

MUSEUM OF DECORATIVE ARTS

In Frankfurt, Germany, the interesting and vigorous expressions of two recent museum additions extend and support original old buildings expected to remain central to the combined work. The first, Richard Meier's Museum of Decorative Arts, succeeds well in principle. The second, Josef Paul Kleihues's Museum of Pre- and Early History, succeeds better in fact.

Richard Meier takes the nearly cubic 1803 Villa Metzler overlooking the River Main as the starting point of his 1979 competition-winning proposal for the expanded Museum of Decorative Arts (fig. 2-27), intending to give the geometry of the old building a pervasive and possibly controlling importance in the geometry of the new whole. The proportions of the Villa's square façade and the pattern of its windows become the source of a grid of small squares that organize the expansion (fig. 2-28). In plan the cube of the Villa itself anchors the corner of the grid, set off by comparably sized new cubes and blocks of space in an L behind and beside it as the only freestanding object in the composition (fig. 2-29). The base grid is then built up with a skewed overlay responding to the difference in ori-

MUSEUM OF DECORATIVE ARTS
Frankfurt, Germany

Villa Metzler, 1803
Richard Meier, 1985

2-27. *The 1803 Villa Metzler at the entry to the Museum of Decorative Arts.*

2-28. *Richard Meier explores the villa as a source of expression*

2-27

2-28

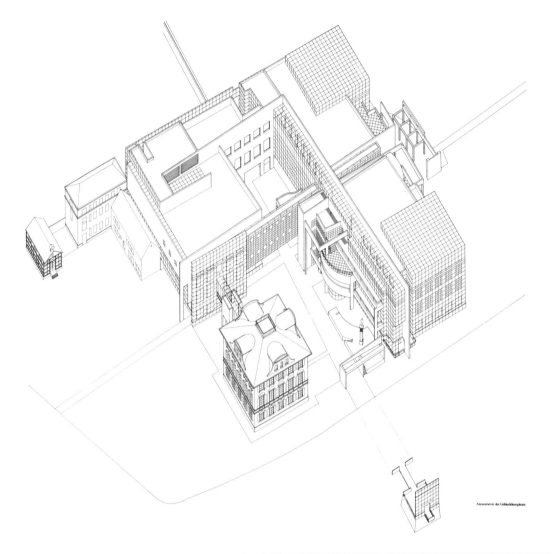

2-29

2-29. *The Villa in the complex composition Meier derives from it*

2-30. *The Villa Metzler and its new neighbor seen from the river*

2-30

44

entation between the Villa on a curve of the street and the straight line of the bulk of the site. The overlay creates an opportunity to distinguish cubes of new space that can be similarly sized and tied directly to the Villa from other spaces shaped, organized, and animated by the interstitial wedges. At the same time the base grid vertically organizes the façades of the addition and provides patterns for Meier's characteristic white metal cladding.

The addition is approximately the height of the Villa. The façade of the end of its L is a square at the scale of the Villa addressing the street and the river like a successor villa (fig. 2-30). The new square façade rises straight out of the ground with windows in number, size, and rhythm like the Villa's, but less adorned (fig. 2-31). It is contained only by the edges of its square without the vertical orientation and closure added by the Villa's conventional base, cornice, dormers, and roof. The combined design is an obvious homage to the Villa, which is the source of its organization, the determiner of the scale of its components, and, standing against the intense modern complexity of the added buildings, the principal piece of craftwork shown off by the expanded museum.

The promise of the scheme is not altogether fulfilled in fact, for reasons that are important in principle and have to do with the interaction and relative strength of the parts in the actual building. The interaction of the old and new is obscured by a screen of big ragged trees left between them. The actual connection between the original building and the addition is a handsome, straight bridge that sticks so forcefully and directly into the middle of the Villa's back as to take away a great part of its autonomy (fig. 2-32). Most important, however strong the old building is as a form, its new neighbors are so much stronger—so big, animated, and full of their own complex geometric business—they seem perfectly content to do

2-31

2-32

2-31. Meier's companion façade

2-32. The bridge connecting old and new

2-33

*2-33. The coigned end gable in
the street façade of Joseph Kleihues's
striped Museum for Pre- and Early
History*

without the Villa, whose neglected paintwork makes it seem forlorn, more tolerated than honored in the composition.

FRANKFURT MUSEUM FOR PRE- AND EARLY HISTORY

Josef Kleihues's Museum for Pre- and Early History gets results that seem more satisfying in part because the Carmelite church to which it attaches is relatively bigger and stronger than the Villa Metzler and in part because the addition to the church is at once more deferential and more intimately allied with it. In Kleihues's collaboration the old church is not just attached to the museum but wrapped into it to serve its purposes (fig. 2-33).

Kleihues's 1989 addition is a straight, slim, striped bar of building that engages and displays the coigned white Gothic end of the church transept as the central and dominant feature of its street wall (fig. 2-34). The bar is solid masonry to close off the street, glazed on the inside to open to the church. The entry is at the end of the bar on a green space dominated by the apse of the church, where a curved glass pavilion attached to the bar helps anchor the addition to the green space and animate its relationship to the church (fig. 2-35). The slender addition squeezes to the side to defer to the church, presenting its smallest dimension as part of the elegantly scaled entry and keeping the church visible in three dimensions at the entry and throughout the new long gallery despite the tightness of the site. The addition borrows the slenderness of the Gothic as the key to its siting and the church's prominent coigns as the source of the stripes that contribute so much to its identity.

Inside the addition actually takes over portions of the church and uses them as parts of its exhibition space (fig. 2-36). One central gallery shows off the church's surviving vaulted roof and another winds old and

46

2-34

2-35

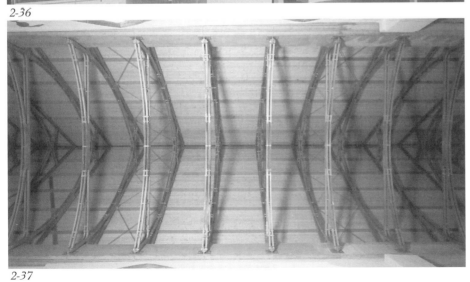

2-36

2-37

2-34. The addition engages the white Carmelite church

2-35. The extended coigns and the glazed connector

2-36. The church in the museum

2-37. The museum contributes to the church

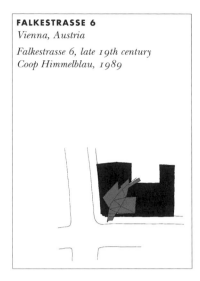

FALKESTRASSE 6
Vienna, Austria

Falkestrasse 6, late 19th century
Coop Himmelblau, 1989

2-38

2-39

2-38. *The elegant catastrophe of Coop Himmelblau's penthouse addition to Falkestrasse 6 in Vienna*

2-39. *Sketch of the angel of built death*

new together with a beautiful new steel vault derived by Kleihues from the old (fig. 2-37). Integrated into the architecture of the museum as a whole, the church becomes an active participant in its work, bringing a context of age that makes the ancient exhibits more accessible. Virtually new relative to the exhibits, the Gothic church contributes an interesting and unusual depth in time to a thoroughly modern combined work.

FALKESTRASSE 6

The expressive resources of abstract contemporary architecture can be applied to serve purposes as artificial and poetic as any served by decorative conventions of prior architecture, extending traditions the modernists might have appeared to repudiate in their disdain for ornament.

The work of the Coop Himmelblau includes the proposition that legitimate expressive results can be derived like aleatory music from random design processes such as psychograms, I Ching sticks, and drawing blindfolded. An early success is the lawyers' office suite superimposed in 1989 on the ordinary office building at Number 6 Falkestrasse in Vienna (fig. 2-38). Here a sketch provoked by a poem (fig. 2-39)—highly relevant, as it turns out—provided the parti for a rooftop assembly of sticks and glass that spills over the parapet of an old building as if to threaten the street below (fig. 2-40). The Coop's provocative addition elevates an ordinary background building in one of the world's great baroque cities into an unexpected manifestation of the survival of the baroque itself.

The addition extends the building, not just literally by adding conference rooms and offices for its lawyer owners, but by doing so in a high-tech sculptural envelope that acts like a baroque ceiling painting or a figural roof sculpture. Thus the great ceiling paintings of baroque palaces and churches open up and connect their interiors to the imagined riots of divine activity in the heavens above. They sometimes likewise bring the riot down into the house so that it begins to upset the architecture. The object is to move and disturb the viewer for pleasure but also to drive home and celebrate the importance of the buildings and their owners, to make clear the direct connections their cardinals and princes believe they enjoy with Christian and mythic heavens. By the end of the nineteenth century the heavens engaged by the ceilings and tops of buildings were no longer the next rungs of a useful power structure—rather, they were Jungian worlds of angels and dragons, of grim forms anticipating war and death, like the giant and menacing pickelstube crowning the roof across the street from Number 6.

On Number 6, the representative of the heavens brought down by the Coop Himmelblau is indeed an angel, but expressly an "angel of built death," a very late twentieth-century representative of a heaven of violent randomness brought crashing down on the roof like a built disaster. Yet how wonderful the disaster is in this case, in itself and because it is an office for lawyers, a heaven-sent representative of the disasters that are these and all lawyers' daily manna (fig. 2-41)! Crashing on the roof just the right angel for their clients, the architects understand and extend for their benefit one of Vienna's particular urban expressive connections, enriching the city and another of its old buildings with a fine piece of contemporary baroque.

ING BANK

Not far from Vienna, in Budapest, as if to keep up a great Austro-Hungarian connection and rivalry, the Dutch architect Erick van Egeraat in 1994 floats in the roof of the restored ING Bank (fig. 2-42) what

2-40

2-41

2-40. The angel contemplates the neighborhood

2-41. Memento mori: inside the angel, the lawyers contemplate a neighbor's pickelstube

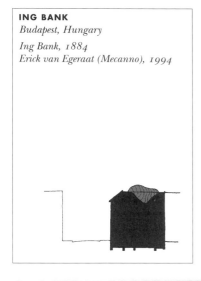

2-42

2-43

2-42. *The ING bank's new acquisition in Budapest*

2-43. *The leviathan, the bankers' great celestial asset*

2-44. *The bankers' heaven*

2-44

its denizens clearly hope to see in their heaven—a huge whalelike form, a monstrous asset cruising their skies (fig. 2-43). Not content to let them see and salivate at what awaits them in heaven, van Egeraat lets the bankers move in (fig. 2-44). What complex complicity in an extension, and what gratification!

Derivation

In another class of additions, the new sets off with a different kind of independence to explore not just the same problem as the original but some of the implications of its expression. It derives its own expression from an elaboration of the expressive possibilities of the original and in so doing maintains a particularly close and respectful relationship with it. By acknowledging the original as the source of its expressive ideas, the new virtually guarantees the original its place at the head of the combined expressive hierarchy.

MAISON DE VERRE

The moment the utterly conventional Parisian porte at 31, Rue Saint-Guillaume clicks open and reveals in the utterly conventional Parisian internal apartment courtyard the wonders of Pierre Chareau's 1928 Maison de Verre is one of the great moments in any experience of architecture. Locked in and under the painted masonry of the courtyard is a pioneering modernist exploration of the functional and expressive possibilities of steel and glass (fig. 2-45). With the fitness of a surgeon's instrument, Chareau's contrivance of light, space, and machinery represents and serves the rare mixture of prominence, intimacy, and exposure of a fashionable home that is a gynecological clinic by day and a salon by night.

50

While the old apartment courtyard itself seems strictly background to the contrivance, it played an important role in the development of the Maison. A third-floor tenant refused to move, so the Maison took its overall form in order to fit under her. The old courtyard set the problem for the new design, the capture and management of light, security, and privacy for the inhabitants of the courtyard's darkest, least private floors and for patients coming for examination and advice. The old architecture—a typical Parisian assembly of painted bearing masonry with curtained windows set deep in blank walls—sets off the radical alternative treatment of the same issues explored and dramatized by Chareau in metal and glass (fig. 2-46).

Chareau gives the doctor's new house a proper prominence in the court by bringing it forward. On the face of the house he shows off a large piece of blank wall, a flat rectangle of vertical surface presented face on to the viewer, built up out of repeated glass units that are relatively opaque. These glass units are not block, like masonry, but structural glass used in floors, a different masonry, a wearing rather than a bearing surface. Against the plain old wall, the new wall stands out for its interest, showing off the graphic pattern of its units and the elegant structure that holds them together. At the same time its translucent glass solves the critical problem for the wall, admitting as much as possible of available light for the health and happiness of the owners while assuring patients that they are not inappropriately exposed.

This capacity of glass in varying degrees to admit and exclude is an important organizing device for the design as a whole. Viewed from the entry to the court, a service wing extends out to the left at right angles to the principal façade. It has horizontal clear glass strip windows that, because they are presented at right angles

MAISON DE VERRE
Paris, France

31, rue Saint-Guillaume, 18th century
Pierre Chareau, 1932

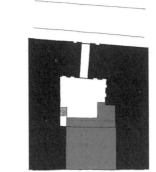

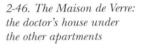

2-45

2-45. Pierre Chareau's Maison de Verre is just discernible through the window of 31, rue Saint-Guillaume, Paris

2-46. The Maison de Verre: the doctor's house under the other apartments

2-46

51

2-47

2-48

2-49

2-50

2-47. Degrees of
transparency:
where you see in,
you go in

2-48. Chareau's
floodlamps pro-
vide light and pri-
vacy at night

2-49. The clinical
light of day

2-50. The glow of
the salon at night

to the viewer, only partially expose the interior. Straight ahead, set back in the shadow
beneath the principal wall of the house, are
two separate planes of glass holding the
entry door at right angles between them
where it cannot be seen (fig. 2-47). The first
of these planes is clear glass and shows the
entry hall: the thing you can see into is the
thing you are supposed to go into, made
important and attractive by the relative
abundance of detail and information visible
through shaded, transparent glass.

An important use of glass to manage light
and privacy comes in the way the glass masonry, more than opaque and less than transparent, literally adumbrates—suggests but does
not reveal—in differing ways and to different
degrees by day and by night, what is going on
inside. The management of this suggestion is
interestingly evident in its provisions for the
lighting of the building at night from the outside. Stanchions and lamps are important
expressive elements in the exterior design of
both the court and garden façades, greatly
enriching the building elevations (fig. 2-48).
The glass wall is a remarkable source of a
cool, clinical north light by day (fig. 2-49).
The incandescent lamps outside produce a
softer equivalent inside at night and, as well,
manage the jack-o'-lantern effect of the
inside lighting. Warmer at night, with the
suggestive shadow of the doctor's piano, the
glass wall displays his salon to the court like a
tapestry (fig. 2-50).

In this play with the capacities of glass to
admit and exclude, the Maison de Verre is an
early exploration of those attributes that
make glass arguably the twentieth century's
greatest addition to architects' expressive
armamentarium. These attributes dramatize
the functions of a wall, given the century's
new technical possibilities, in an intimate
urban context where the capacities of glass
are both intriguing and effective. Like the old
walls that show off its novelty, the new wall still
holds things up but with its bearing function

abstracted out, transferred to steel and exposed, and with all its remaining functions transferred to glass. Glass now generally holds things out—rain, air, light, and visitors—and controls their admission. Like the curtains and shutters of the old wall, it manages privacy and security within the rich range tolerated in a Paris courtyard, animating the resulting composition by what it does and does not reveal of the private lives it serves.

HUBERTUS HOUSE

Aldo van Eyck's 1979 addition to the Hubertus House, a home for single mothers in Amsterdam, expands a relatively conventional masonry townhouse on the Plantage Middenlaan near the Amsterdam Zoo (fig. 2-51). The addition attaches to the old house by a recessed stair tower, partially filled by a two-story piece of frame and tracery put next to the old house as if to lock onto it. The connector sorts out the different floor-to-floor heights between the old and the new and organizes the combined elevation, marking out the portion of the new façade that is proportioned like a townhouse and balancing it against the old townhouse itself. The connector creates for the institution a closely integrated double entry adapted to its social purposes: the official entry up the old stoop and a discreet way to the same stair in the shadow of the connector.

Across the recess from the solid, reflective light-gray masonry plane of the old house van Eyck sets a delicate metal frame façade that takes in light through its abundant glass. Where the reflective masonry of the old house is ornamented with brackets and pendentives and divided lights, the absorbent glass of the addition is divided with tracery, including three arches derived from a real arch in the cornice of the old house, a decorative introduction to a complex assembly of sticks.

The composition of the old façade is rela-

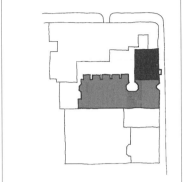

HUBERTUS HOUSE
Amsterdam, The Netherlands

Hubertus House, 19th century
Aldo van Eyck, 1979

2-51. Hubertus House in Amsterdam with Aldo van Eyck's metal and glass addition

2-52. The living spaces of the addition tumble out the back

2-51

2-52

tively upright and vertical. The components of the addition are relatively horizontal, trailing away to the side. Where the old façade firmly occupies its place as a stable and complete vertical rectangle with three even rows of four large, solid, vertical rectangular windows—a rhythm of twos—the addition divides its three bays into one, two, and three lights successively, a more elusive play of twos and threes. The center line of the old house is strongly marked with a central arch and a single high central window in its cornice, two special central windows in the piano nobile, and an ornate balcony centered beneath the two of them. On the ground floor the stoop and the official front door knock the composition just a little off-center. The addition picks up on this asymmetry in its apparent bay widths, the two against three of its glazing, the heights of its cornices at two-and-a-half, three, and four stories, and the deeply shadowed off-center private entry in the recess. Behind the different façades the buildings confirm the cues they give. The old house is redeveloped regularly within its bearing walls and square footprint. The addition throws out relatively loosely into the yard to the rear like a toss of pickup sticks, a long tail of repeating bedrooms, playrooms, and special spaces for various forms of nurture (fig. 2-52). When the addition was virtually complete, van Eyck made his famous decision to paint its metal in many colors, once again setting off the flat plain-white reflective front of the old against the cheerfully multicolored but nevertheless darker, shadowed, more introverted addition.

In his derivation of elements of connection, contrast, and hierarchy in the expression of his addition, van Eyck manages the relationship of the new and the old within the institution and at the same time brings out the institution as a whole in its time and within the context of its street. The old house is by itself a comforting manifestation of old-fashioned charity, the generous provision of a home for poor people that also bundles them off out of sight behind a façade of *bürgerlich* convention. The addition reflects the willingness of its times to talk rather more openly about the issues, about the poor themselves, about prostitutes as mothers, about their children, about their need to slip off the street into a shelter that is private and cheerful. By maintaining the original home at the head of the composition in the plane of the street, then adding beside it the light-absorbing façade and the shadowed entry into the colorful protective folds of the interior, van Eyck honors the institution for its history and its current service, giving it distinct new weight on its street and in its neighborhood.

The buildings' combined evocation of charitable ideals has been affected in recent years by further social change. As part of the global lowering of expectations with respect to social service, the Hubertus House as an institution has been absorbed into a larger municipal system and the functions to which its buildings were so finely tuned dispersed or abandoned. Now only a last few mothers and children hang on as the building is gradually and rather awkwardly converted to offices. On a heavily traveled all-business street, Van Eyck's subtle and delicate presentation of an architecture of human service seems more than a bit forlorn.

500 PARK AVENUE

For more than thirty years, the Pepsi-Cola Building of Skidmore Owings Merrill's Gordon Bunshaft has stood with Lever House and the Seagram Building as one of the three finest manifestations of the International Style in America—and one of the finest of New York City's limited stock of distinguished works of modern architecture (fig. 2-53).

The Pepsi-Cola Building is organized to make the most of the limited inherent expressive possibilities of a small quantity of corporate office space, presented as an elegantly proportioned rectangular block set on edge and and clearly defined by a set-back ground floor, a set-back penthouse, and black reveals on the sides. The narrow, vertical, and relatively active east elevation of the block faces Park Avenue; the broader, square, and stable north elevation, which actually has the entry, faces 59th Street. Two columns are exposed at the base of the east end as if to give weight to Park Avenue in the competition of the two façades in the building's very subtle formal hierarchy.

The two façades are clad in a curtain wall of the utmost simplicity, combining the flattest possible horizontal aluminum panels and the slenderest possible vertical aluminum mullions with the largest possible horizontal rectangles of Belgian plate glass. The metal of the façades orders them in modules that balance square and rectangular and horizontal and vertical. Only the slim vertical mullions have depth and shadow, as if to help them balance in importance the broad, flat horizontals. The rectangular plates of clear glass held by the metal complete an envelope notable for its virtual nonexistence. Through it the building's structure and its stacked floors read like Le Corbusier's Domino House diagram, the floors reduced at night by luminous ceilings to a stack of planes of light (fig. 2-54). The whole is an elegant downtown icon of the international corporate ideal of its time—transparent, colorless, placeless, and almost without particular identity, but beautifully formed and animated nevertheless by a finely equilibrated balance of significant tensions.

The still youthful, unprotected building faced demolition in the late 1970s, being small for its site. Instead, its expansion became possible when a sympathetic owner joined it with a neighbor to the west, adding ground for a tower that could rise beside and then cantilever partially over it. In the combined 500 Park, Pepsi-Cola's commercial

500 PARK AVENUE
New York, New York

Skidmore Owings & Merrill, 1960
James Stewart Polshek & Partners, 1985

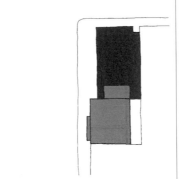

2-53. The Pepsi-Cola Building in New York: Skidmore Owings and Merrill's Pazzi Chapel of corporate design

2-54. The building at night as corporate DOMINO House

2-53

2-54

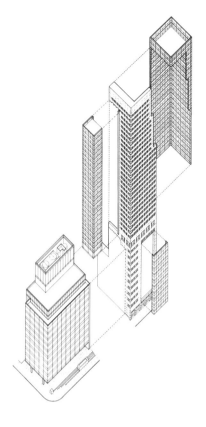

2-55

2-56

floors expanded laterally into the new base, with apartments above them in the tower.

At the corner of 59th Street and Park Avenue, 500 Park stood at a fairly clear border between uses with their own conventions of architectural expression: smooth, reductive International Style metal and glass curtain walls on the headquarter offices to the south, and rougher, older masonry walls with smaller molded or incised openings and some abiding domestic warmth on the apartment buildings to the north. The new building starts from the delicate balance of Pepsi-Cola's curtain wall, adapting it for the enclosure of the extension of the office space into the tower, then winding the new transparent white-metal wall in with a contrasting opaque dark granite masonry surface punched with windows. In the masonry wall, the granite is flame finished and rough and the window openings are shadowed by deep stone returns to make sure the granite reads as masonry, not just another form of curtain wall, and keeps the residential association. The corner of the masonry surface is brought all the way to the ground to anchor the combination and mark the residential entry. At the joint the Pepsi-Cola elevation runs into the descending surface of the tower almost unrevealed, emphasizing the continuity of the extension but also reproducing some of the tensions of its own delicate balance. Beyond the joint, the new curtain wall—even more reduced than the old and still more elegant—spirals up around the axis of the tower, becoming prominent in the cantilever over Pepsi-Cola and finally topping off the building. The two expressions remain corporate, cool, and colorless, but now defined and intertwined on the surface of an active, warmer form amplified from the energy balanced in the Pepsi-Cola building (fig. 2-55).

The result is an unusual extension of the coolest of corporate expressions to fit what is now a commercial speculation in costly executive residences. A rare tall building that makes sense of the form with something other than the conventional bottom, middle, and top, 500 Park has some of the strangeness of truly original work (fig. 2-56), an experimental or adolescent gangliness in the way it twists the old and the new together around its axis and finally balances over the old building. Pepsi-Cola remains the lead object in the composition, transparent and white against the dark stone background of the tower. It gives up autonomy but gains permanence and status as the obvious progenitor of a complex response both to it and to its setting.

THE MAISON CARRÉE AND THE CARRÉ D'ART

Norman Foster's 1991 Carré d'Art, the large municipal art museum at Nîmes, occupies the fourth side of the urban enclosure developed over the years by the city for its world-class Roman antiquity, the dense, definitional lump of classicism of the Maison Carrée (fig. 2-57). Here Foster's scheme refills the footprint and restores the bulk of a nineteenth-century opera house that was part of the monument's familiar setting (fig. 2-58). The opera itself burned down, leaving its colonnade as the façade of a parking lot. Refilling the site, the new building reestablishes the familiar setting with a replacement object derived with great sensitivity and intelligence from the Maison Carrée. The result is provoking in its strength but also richly illuminating, as it shows off the old building not just as a monument but as a resource.

Foster's proposal for the Carré d'Art remained the same in many respects throughout the progress from his winning design to the final building. It always refilled the opera site with a regular, rectangular companion block addressing the regular rectangular Maison Carrée at right

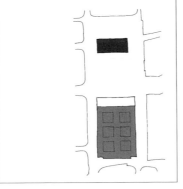

MAISON CARRÉE AND THE CARRÉ D'ART
Nîmes, France
Maison Carrée, 1st Century B.C.
Foster Associates, 1991

2-57. *The Maison Carrée with Foster and Partners' Carré d'Art in Nîmes*

2-58. *The Maison Carrée and the Nîmes Opera before the opera house burned*

2-57

2-58

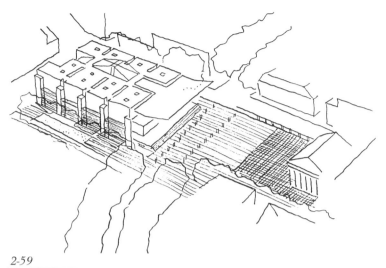

2-59

2-60

2-61

angles (fig. 2-59). Much of the new volume was sunk below ground to keep the new roofline near the height of the rooftops of Nîmes. A passage through the building kept open a major pedestrian footway between the monuments of the city. What evolved were the ways the new building actually engaged the monument. At the start, Foster intended his kindred object to take it on directly: he removed the opera colonnade. The winning scheme directed its attention to the Maison with a high, flared marquee and two abstract stone correlatives of the old building (fig. 2-60) brought under its protection. The opera colonnade, however, had friends enough to make the mayor ask Foster to try to save it, and Foster's next proposal duly put it back. Instead of asking to be considered with the Maison Carrée, the new building took cover behind the colonnade, leaving the monument alone in a simulacrum of the old Temple Square, recoddled in the familiar (fig. 2-61). Then, with a mixture of courage and practicality, the mayor changed his mind and abandoned the colonnade, reopening the question of how the new building should address the Maison Carrée. As consolation to its friends, the disembodied colonnade was enshrined against the Mediterranean sky in the landscape of a rest stop on the Autoroute.

Foster's next schemes gave up the notion of showing off something new or old opposite the Maison, exploring instead a variety of recessive forms that would accommodate the entry to the new building and the ancient skewed path of travel through it and through the site. Variations on a shallow glass triangular funnel now took in the space of the square, as if yielding to the importance of the old monument (fig. 2-62) and the traditional itinerary through the site. Foster considered different contributions his projecting roof might make as a device to help the connection. The first, flared like a trumpet, offered the Maison something of a fanfare. Succeeding schemes dropped the fanfare, making the projection purely a sheltering trellis for what it put on show underneath. Schemes like the funnel scheme dropped the cover altogether. In what became the final design, the marquee came back, transformed by slim vertical tie rods into a portico like the Maison's (fig. 2-63) The Carré d'Art now appeared across from the Maison Carrée with its kinship made obvious by the portico, lines of derivation from the monument multiplied, pulled tighter, and made more explicit as the principal connecting device.

As a rectangle with its axis toward the square, the Carré d'Art addresses the side of the Maison Carrée, neither competing with nor reinforcing its orientation, making it and its ancient relationship to the city together the object of its attention. The Maison Carrée goes about its ghostly business, offering its beauty to the city and to its gods as it has for two millennia. Addressing it from its position as something to the side, the recognizably similar Carré d'Art makes a comparable offer with respect to art but at a remove like a descendant, the ancestral elements all in place but transformed by twentieth-century technical and tectonic possibilities (fig. 2-64). The relationships are pervasive. They start with the steps and portico—low, quick steps, not the hard climb up stone blocks to the Maison Carrée, and a portico so lightly drawn as almost to be implied, a metal shade for an off-center entry and the survivor of the original abstract correlative blocks (fig. 2-65). Supported by minimal metal ties, the portico is the slimmest offspring of the robust, entatic columns of the Maison Carrée, a block of air rather than the forest of air and masonry across the street. Overall, like the Maison, the Carré d'Art exists to house a central place of worship. Up its steps and through its portico is a central court with a glorious,

2-62

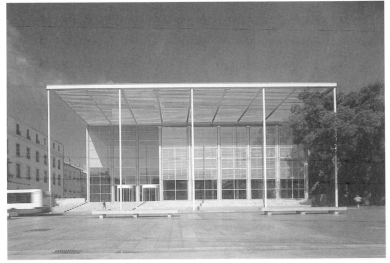

2-63

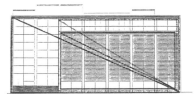

2-64

2-59. Sketch for the proposed building and its relationship to the monument

2-60. Model of the winning design displays objects under a marquee

2-61. Trying out the possibility of reusing the opera façade

2-62. A recessive proposal backs off altogether from the monument

2-63. The portico establishes the final attachment by kinship

2-64. Kindred proportions

2-65

2-65. *The entry to the new temple*

2-66. *The equivalent of the old sacred space*

2-67. *The venerable ancestor visible from inside*

2-66

2-67

glowing glass stair that leads to its various shrines of the arts and information (fig. 2-66). The walls that enclose its court are flat and unbroken like the Maison's side walls, similarly marked out and proportioned and, in part, similarly exclusive. Now, however, they are perfectly transparent, not perfectly opaque, protecting the sacred space but allowing it to be seen and illuminated.

While comparable elements make the connection with the monument, the way they are used in the expression of the new building has the effect of moving them down the hierarchy from the perfect, dense integrity with which they are presented in the original. Masonry, for example, is gone from the Carré d'Art. The solid, excluding Mediterranean stone belongs to the Maison and to antiquity. The Carré's walls are laid up and proportioned by lines of metal structure and the grids of shades not unlike masonry but are instead a receptive, clear, very twentieth-century glass. The descent is not seamless; the size of the Carré d'Art and the strength of its portico seem almost enough to break it off, to set the Carré up as a high modernist competitor rather than a successor. Then the remarkable lightness and transparency of its metal and glass redeem it; the Carré d'Art is pervaded not just with the Maison's ideas but with the image of the real thing (fig. 2-67).

IRCAM

Renzo Piano's inventive 1989 addition to his earlier IRCAM (Centre Internationale de Recherche Acoustique et Musique), the underground Music Research Center of the Centre Pompidou in Paris (fig. 2-68), extends and humanizes the assertions the original makes about music as a participant in the Pompidou's outspoken public advocacy of the arts.

Piano's original 1975 IRCAM was represented by a perfect rectangular void

2-68

2-68. Renzo Piano's addition to the IRCAM brings it up to the surface and ties it into the neighborhood in Paris

2-69. The original void of the Place Stravinsky announcing the IRCAM

2-69

2-70

2-71

2-70. *Under the void Piano and Rogers's severe façade cheered up by giant graffiti*

2-71. *The void at the bottom, the Espace de Projection, a great room for music*

announcing its reduced inversion of the main building of the Centre Pompidou (fig. 2-69). The void, the new Place Stravinsky, was clearly defined by buildings on the sides, by the perfectly flat façade of the IRCAM at the bottom (fig. 2-70) and by the empty sky above. The entry to the IRCAM was a slot in the floor of the Place covered with flat glass, with an opening for the single-run staircase—like the Pompidou's but going down into the ground—simply dropping out of the void. Underground was a block of concrete and glass studios all opening onto the staircase as it led to the ultimate void at the bottom, the Espace de Projection (fig. 2-71).

Like the main building of the Pompidou, the IRCAM is a remarkable architectural discussion of the art it serves. The music pursued at the IRCAM is literally out of this world, to be sought in perfect silence underground and rendered in the Espace de Projection—a mystery appropriately announced by the void of the Place Stravinsky. The gargantuan flared ventilators sticking up from below along the side of the Place Stravinsky have a certain humor as reminders of the activity below and that the workers—nibelungen, perhaps—need to breathe. Within the building underground, however, all was the highest of high seriousness like the music being pursued in what was, particularly in the Espace de Projection, the twentieth century's finest marriage of architecture and acoustics.

The IRCAM was always under pressure to lighten up—witness the graffiti or the installation of the pool and cheery statues that made the Place Stravinsky into an attraction more like the rest of the Centre. The addition came at a time when the actual yield from the IRCAM's intense pursuit of music was considered by some to be slim—a good time perhaps to come up for air and join the neighborhood. On the surface Piano ran into bourgeois constraints; the local authorities required that his addition be brick, to fit with the old brick buildings around it. He also found opportunities—notably in the interesting façade of the adjacent old school building with its proto-Pompidou external stair detail stepping down across its glazed face (fig. 2-72)—and in the fact that the addition could occupy a prominent corner with two sides exposed to the Place Pompidou.

Asked for brick, Piano delivers brick, but what brick!—beautiful, long, thin orange-red roman brick set not in mortar but hung in panels of stainless steel (fig. 2-73), brick indeed but brick exhibited as a part of an exploded technology of enclosure, as a source of a satisfying rhythm, color, and texture, and as a participant in a rain screen, nothing more. He then stacks up the brick panels uninterrupted on both sides of his corner to a height above the old buildings but lower than the Pompidou, a colorful, reflective turning post, an advanced technology of enclosure held up in its opacity and imperviousness against the airy exterior of the Pompidou.

At the corner the red oblong of the tower (fig. 2-74) now announces the IRCAM with a more accessible but still disciplined reminder of the work going on in the isolation below, the beautifully ordered blank of the panels, like the original void, representing and protecting the mystery of the IRCAM's musical pursuit. Now, however, the severe technical modernity of the tower ties directly into the bourgeoiserie of the Bains Douches facing the Place Pompidou and into the old school facing the Place Stravinsky. Connecting the tower and the school are new elevators and a plane of glass and steel. The plane of glass continues the plane of brick of the corner, subdivided in panels and with plates of glass substituted for the brick. The glass completes the development of the façade of the school (now the IRCAM library) and accepts the downward movement of its charming what's-so-novel-about-

2-72

2-73

2-72. The entry to the IRCAM addition with the proto-Pompidou stair feeding in from the old library

2-73. Piano's answer to the city's requirement that the building be brick

2-74. The tower's blankness maintains some of the original mystery

2-74

63

2-75

the-big-Pompidou-escalator? stair. Access to the new entry from the Place Stravinsky crosses over the slot for the IRCAM's original descending stair on a short arched bridge, the new route superimposed with humor across the portentous original descent into the earth.

Piano's addition compromises his original in one important respect: with the new entry, the top flights of the descending stair are no longer necessary and are removed, weakening its great progress toward the Espace de Projection and blurring the IRCAM's internal architecture into something less rigorous and more ordinary. At the same time, the addition enhances the IRCAM's connections to the Centre Pompidou and to its neighborhood. With the post at the corner, the public space is clarified and a very important part of the monumental Centre marked. The Pompidou newly illuminates the possibilities of the architectural ideas it set out to exhibit and explore. And the IRCAM's connection to the ordinary world is improved with a respectful but significantly humanized self-advertisement in the Pompidou's argument for the arts.

All good things, of course, must come to an end (fig. 2-75). In a subsequent renovation, not by the Renzo Piano Building Workshop, the old library was reworked to serve the IRCAM and, in an unnecessary act of remarkable obtuseness, the step-stair removed. Alas!

Transformation

Sometimes the new sets out with the expressed intention of operating upon the meaning of the old, not necessarily to alter it but rather to restate it with a new order of force. Some of the projects in France—collectively known as the Grands Projets—illustrate such transformations particularly well.

These projects are all explicitly a form of urban renewal, one that winds up not with destructive wastelands but with buildings that vindicate an enviable commitment of public resources to serious architecture as a tool for urban betterment. Central examples are Piano and Rogers's Centre Pompidou, Pei's alteration of the Louvre, and Nouvel's reconstruction of the Lyon Opera House. In Berlin, Foster's evolving proposal for the Reichstag shows two versions of such a transformation, what it might have been and what it will become.

CENTRE POMPIDOU

The 1974 Centre Pompidou is an example of these transformations at the largest scale, where a new expression operates on an entire city—in this case, Paris—and indeed on an entire nation (fig. 2-76).

When it appeared, the Centre Pompidou was like nothing anyone had seen before. Imposed on the city with all the assertive novelty of its obvious ancestors, the Eiffel Tower and the Grand Palais, the Centre was (and remains) the most enthusiastic public celebration of what buildings do ever provoked by modernism—the innards of architecture stood up and made vivid like a plate in an anatomy book (fig. 2-77). Its grandstand demonstration of a twentieth-century building at work (fig. 2-78), its inviting galleries, and its remarkable public library made it an attraction even more magnetic than both prior festival celebrations of French technical and artistic achievement.

The mighty rectangular box of the Centre in fact fitted the dense blocks of the city more closely than did its ancestors, a piece of the city rather than a piece apart in a park. Traced in outline, filled out with structural pieces, mechanical equipment, and, within them, the actual glass wall of its enclosed spaces, it offered a (super)abundance of detail readable at the scale of the

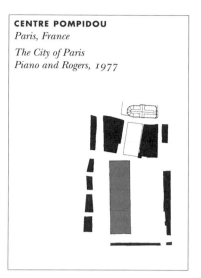

CENTRE POMPIDOU
Paris, France

The City of Paris
Piano and Rogers, 1977

2-76. The Centre Pompidou: a vast new monument in the city of Paris

2-76

65

2-77. *The Centre's architectural anatomy lesson*

2-78. *The building as spectacle*

2-79. *The Centre in the Paris roofscape*

2-77

2-78

2-79

buildings around it. Its open spaces were comparable to others in its neighborhood, not parks but "places" walled by buildings. The Centre pushed up substantially above its neighborhood, enough to be recognized as a monument, like the naves of churches, but still an intimate fit with the city's roofscape (fig. 2-79).

As a national museum of modern art, the Pompidou makes vivid what it thinks an art museum should do and be with its warehouse of galleries, its supporting tubes and wires, and its energetic display of an architecture of progress and entertainment, an exciting kind of popular worship. It winds together the attachments of its two architects to divergent traditions, Piano's to the complexities of the building envelope as a Renaissance instrument of human service and Rogers's to the same complexities as a baroque device to impress and entertain. Scaled to act at the grandest level upon the national capital and the national self-esteem, the Pompidou is a strong, cheerful, and effective demonstration of human artistic and mechanical intelligence that transforms Paris's built celebration of national achievement with a demonstration of technical prowess appropriate for its time.

LOUVRE PYRAMID, PALAIS DU LOUVRE

I. M. Pei's 1993 glass pyramid, the biggest new object in the Louvre (fig. 2-80), completes the transformation of the Palais du Louvre into a proper seat of contemporary French power.

As a seat of political power, the Louvre was anchored by Claude Perrault's commanding classical east façade (fig. 2-81), imposed by Louis XIV on the earlier Cour Henri II. The Cour Henri II in turn anchored two long, pendant wings of evolving shapes and lengths that embraced the garden of the Cour du Louvre. As it grew in public importance as a museum, the Louvre's effective entry shifted

LOUVRE PYRAMID, PALAIS DU LOUVRE
Paris, France

Palais du Louvre, 12th to 19th centuries
I. M. Pei & Partners, 1993

2-80. I. M. Pei's Pyramid in the Musée du Louvre

2-80

2-81

2-82

2-83

away from Perrault's façade to the open-ended Cour (fig. 2-82), which filled with cars. Dropped into the Cour, the large glass pyramid rebalanced the composition in favor of the museum. A bright, strong, clear, stable, centered geometrical form in the middle of what had become an indeterminate open space, the pyramid took command of the Cour and required all the surrounding parts—wings, connections, and open space—to acknowledge that they in served a single, powerful master. In the embrace of the wings, the freestanding pyramid offered itself as an explanatory precious object to stand for the collection that gives the Louvre its importance (fig. 2-83). And it fixed itself at the climax of the axial march of triumphal objects—the Arc de la Défense, the Arc de Triomphe, the Carrousel du Louvre—by which France now celebrates the power not of its armies but of its history, its culture, and its art.

The pyramid is a rewarding application of Pei's interest in pure geometrical forms to a specific task. Pei was not the first to see the value of the form in itself or as an organizing device in the center of the Cour du Louvre (fig. 2-84). In his hands, however, the pure form is particularly readable. It evokes obvious associations with grand axial French garden design, with masonic emblems of occult knowledge and illumination, and with the Louvre as a repository of national treasure; with the great geometrical forms adopted at the end of the eighteenth century for architectural celebrations of greatness and mortality like Boulée's tomb of Newton; and with the great collector, Napoleon, whose victory in Egypt under the eye of the pyramids' twenty centuries associated them with French *gloire*.

The glass pyramid in itself completes the Louvre's sustained evolution from massive fortress to glittering international attraction. Underneath Pei's pyramid is the massive windowless masonry of Philip le Bel's first assertion of French power in Paris.

2-84

2-85

2-86

2-81. The beginning of the development of the present Louvre, Claude
Perrault's expression of French power
at its zenith

2-82. Before the pyramid, the Cour
du Louvre was exposed as an indeterminate space

2-83. The pyramid takes charge

2-84. An earlier pyramid occupied
the same spot

2-85. Contrasting "masonry":
the hard pyramid and the fleshy
Pavillon Sully

2-86. The pyramid at the head
of a sequence of French triumphs

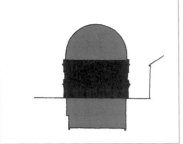

2-87. *The Lyon Opera: a powerful new partnership*

2-88. *Chenavard and Pollet's old opera house before Jean Nouvel's addition*

2-89. *Nouvel's half-cylinder resolves the arcaded rectangle around a line*

2-90. *The tympanum of the new opera with the roofs of the Hôtel de Ville*

Around it is a graduated sequence of walls from Perrault's classic façade to Visconti and LeFuel's parade of the fleshy goods of Napoleon III (fig. 2-85). In the sequence the balance of material gradually shifts from stone to glass, from one kind of show to another. At the end is the ultimate symbol of stone masonry, the pyramid, made into one big, glazed opening. Like its ancestor, the Maison de Verre, the pyramid expresses in glass a new balance of invitation and exclusion, its mass all but replaced by space. Compression within it exists only to equilibrate tension, opacity replaced by transparency and the gemlike emblem of impenetrability and resistance becoming the single bright signpost for entry.

The pyramid's definitive form and wealth of associations ends any ambiguity about the Louvre. It also makes almost too explicit a claim about power and immortality. With the pyramid in place, the Louvre is not just a former palace or a disused seat of government with pictures in it; it is the culmination and resolution of the great axis of the Republic in the palace provided by France for the art collection that continues to guarantee it a place in the world (fig. 2-86).

LYON OPERA HOUSE

Jean Nouvel's 1993 expansion of Chenavard and Pollet's 1830 Lyon Opera House refills an architectural landmark with a powerful new geometrical form (fig. 2-87), this time not so much to help it serve a new master as to restore it to a prominence once enjoyed by J. G. Soufflot's pioneering 1780 theater, its ancestor on the site.

Soufflot's theater was the first of many to become major participants in the organization of their cities. The successor house was embedded in the city near a river edge, a pendant to Hardouin Mansart's fine, long Hotel de Ville and, through the Hotel de Ville, to the city's finest open space, the Place Belle-

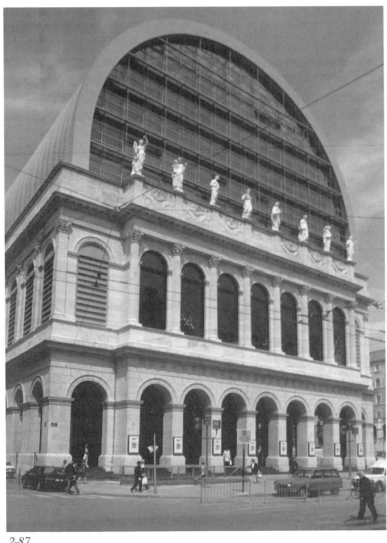

2-87

cour. Simple and strong in its form, detached just enough to be read as an autonomous solid, the opera house maintained the claim of Soufflot's theater to a place in its city like that of cathedrals and palaces.

At the time Nouvel expanded it, Chenavard and Pollet's opera house had so far declined in urban importance that it was not even mentioned by Michelin (fig. 2-88). Both the needs of the Opéra and the scale of the city had changed. To make the opera house work again for both its art and its city, Nouvel gutted Chenavard's arcade and refilled it with an entirely new interior block of building. The new block began below the old walls and rose up through and above them to end in a huge metal and glass half-cylinder at least as high as the height of the original building. The half-cylinder addition projects Chenavard's base rectangle to enlarge its volume. At the same time, with the springline of its curve exactly at the roofline of the old walls, the half-cylinder resolves and closes it the way a dome might, but with a simpler geometry derived from and controlled by the geometry of the rectangle below (fig. 2-89). The half-cylinder presents a unified, low-relief surface plainer than the rich, white, classically arched and decorated old masonry walls below. Its surface and structure is subdivided in a rhythm directly dependent on the rhythm of the colonnade. The transparency of its glass is a development of the windows and arches in the old masonry, extending its display of the activities of the interior as part of the Opéra's public show.

The simplicity of Nouvel's geometry gives it great power. From the urban point of view the result is remarkable. The orientation of the opera house's long form reaffirms its pendency to the Hotel de Ville, its flat, half-circular end section a strong backup to its roofs (fig. 2-90) and, at the head of the sequence, the equestrian relief of Henri IV on the tympanum on the Place Bellecour.

2-88

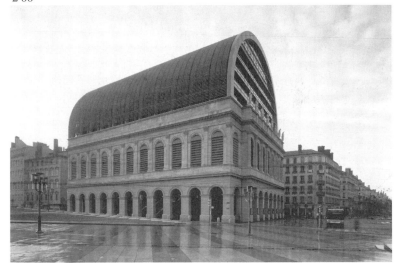

2-89

2-90

71

2-91. The opera behind the Hôtel de Ville, with the king just visible on the tympanum of the Hôtel

2-92. The opera at its most operatic

2-91

2-92

The gray cylinder rises up out of the relatively uniform height of the nineteenth-century central city simple and strong, the biggest single form in its profile (fig. 2-91).

Most important, however, is the way the power of the addition brings out the strength of the original. Simplified and set off by the new deep, black shadow provided all around the base, the rhythmical white arcaded form of the old building is brought out as the controlling presence in the combination, the obvious progenitor of the new form. Above the old shell, the half-cylinder rises and rounds back down to it, deferring formally just enough so that in their burly, tightly united combined expression the old remains the respected and still very active senior partner, like two big singers with their arms around each other letting fly at the end of the act.

As if to bring out the theater in what is going on, Nouvel hangs in the arches lamps that burn red at night like lamps at the door of Falstaff's bordello (fig. 2-92). The color device used here and elsewhere in the night-lighting of the Opéra can be enjoyed for itself and as a humorous and operatic enrichment. At the same time the whore-house metaphor is disturbingly apt for the high-tech orgy of Nouvel's new interior.

THE REICHSTAG

The decision to return the German capital to Berlin carried with it the need to figure out what to do with the hulk of the Reichstag (fig. 2-93), a ruin as freighted with meaning as any surviving the two last European wars. Originally designed by Paul Wallot in a lumpish Imperial baroque as overbearing and self-important as its founding kaiser, as a German interpretation of the imperialism of Chicago's Columbian Exposition (fig. 2-94), it was uplifted thereafter by successive apotheoses of abuse—by Nazi arsonists and by American aviators and Sovi-

72

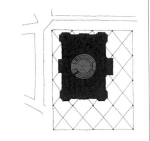

REICHSTAG
Berlin, Germany

Paul Wallot, 1894
Sir Norman Foster and Partners, 1998

2-94

2-93

2-95

2-93. At work on the addition
to the Reichstag, Berlin

2-94. Kaiser Wilhelm's Imperial
Reichstag

2-95. The Reichstag after the war

et infantrymen killing and being killed by children of the Hitler Youth (fig. 2-95). The powerful surviving symbol demanded accommodation in any reestablishment of public power in Berlin. The architectural competition to suggest how to do so focused on its use as a home for the German legislature, the embodiment of the German commitment to democracy. Each of the three finalists gave the former ruin a different place in the hierarchy of the resulting combined work. Pi De Bruijn's scheme filled the Reichstag with offices and located the assembly hall in an egg-shaped addition on

73

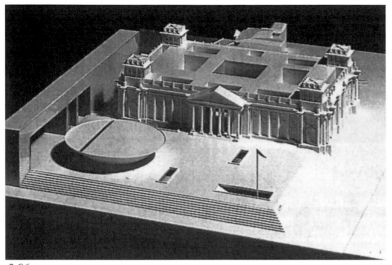

2-96. The Reichstag backing up the legislature in De Bruijn's proposal

2-97. The Reichstag containing the legislature in Santiago Calatrava's proposal

an adjacent plaza, offering a fresh start for the legislature and the downgrading of the Reichstag itself to office space (fig. 2-96). Santiago Calatrava's scheme put the legislature squarely back in the center of the restored ruin but under a soaring lotus-blossom central dome that seemed strong enough to assure a clean, poetic new structure—the built representative of the newest Germany—a controlling place in the combination (fig. 2-97).

Norman Foster's winning design raised the whole matter onto a different plane of significance. Lifting on slender, regular columns over the Reichstag and its immediate site a strange, large, light rectangular roof or canopy, Foster protected and celebrated the ruin like an object in an archeological site with a gargantuan exhibit case implied around it (fig. 2-98). The case called out the special significance of the former ruin and managed its effects by miniaturization, the way Rabelais's giants by comparison made humans small and human nastiness a comedy.

The canopy was also offered as an exploration of the technology of the roof, splitting its functions between canopy and building, using its semishelter to create an intermediate environment for the new seat of government, an outdoor room in which the new government and the relic of the old could work out their new destiny. The canopy invoked technology as a third player greater than either the old or the new. It stood back from and above the actuality of government, putting that actuality within the protection and power of the potential for betterment it reminds us we have.

On consideration, Foster's proposal came to seem too much. After an interim design for a reduced canopy, he was obliged to abandon his gargantuan third player and rebalance the combination in two parts, a technically sophisticated new dome for the legislative chamber emerging from the old building to invoke the same realities and possibilities in a more modest and familiar form (fig. 2-99). The old Reichstag came back into a stronger but more ordinary position in the resulting combination, less symbolic artifact and more potentially useful masonry.

Ultimately the work proceeded as a renovation project of great though less dramatic ingenuity. Details of the building's larger significance—like the interior graffiti from the ghastly last days' fighting of World War II—were protected, while the new and the old were fitted together as a serviceable seat of government. Like the historic move of the German capital back to Berlin, the project evolved from a grand gesture to a piece of hard work.

Across the range of these examples, architects in the modernist descent take on existing buildings and contexts with very different expressive tools and intentions. The intellectual and rhetorical interests of Venturi, for example, lead to very different kinds of engagement with old works than do the formal explorations of Meier, Foster, and Piano. In each addition, however, whatever its expressive agenda, the expressive identity of the original building—the particular meaning it conveyed—is clearly understood and used in a way that correctly reflects its importance and its possibilities as a contributor to the new combined work. Taken together, the examples clearly confirm that a wide variety of expressions can be successfully combined. What matters is not the use of any particular architectural expression but how it is used in the combination.

As to how the new expression should be used, the examples seem to confirm that it is vital to understand the values that are engaged and to be willing to allow those values to have a major role—possibly even a controlling role—in the outcome. In working successfully with these design problems, intelligence and sympathy count.

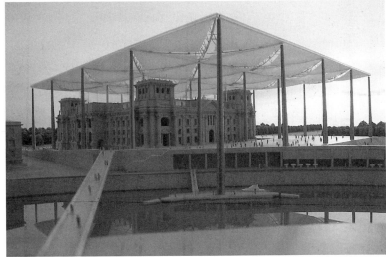

2-98

2-99

2-98. The Reichstag as a highly significant object

2-99. The more modest evocation of contemporary possibilities that is under construction

75

3-1. Stephen Wright's elegant 1758 addition refaced the Cambridge University Old Schools to be a better neighbor for the adjacent 1730 Senate House by James Gibbs

3 Twentieth-Century Combined Works and the Law: The Special Case of Preservation

The examples in the previous chapter illustrate a range of satisfying combined works derived from some of the twentieth century's more interesting expressive explorations. They leave open the narrower judgment whether in any particular combination the original expression can be said to have been preserved (fig. 3-1). The issue here is more focused and technical: in cases where a public interest has attached to a particular expression, does its treatment in the combination reflect and protect that public interest? This judgment demands a certain level of recognition of the protected identity in the combined work, to see that it enjoys the position it deserves because of its acknowledged public worth, and to do so on the basis of a rational, communicable principle enforceable by law.

The Legal Background

Laws protecting the public worth of architectural expression are relatively new. In the United States, the first significant exercises of public power in its favor came in the 1930s in Massachusetts and Louisiana. The bulk of them, including the most important, the New York City Landmarks Preservation Law, were enacted in the 1960s and 1970s.

Enacted in the name of historic preservation, these laws list a variety of consequential public benefits, including the encouragement of tourist revenues and the protection of property values. As the source of these goods, the laws seek to preserve old buildings and other fixed artifacts and objects found by various criteria to be historic. In protecting under this rubric what is largely old architecture, they protect certain experiences having public value, experiences available only if the architecture remains in place and the public can walk around and look at it. The laws fundmen-

tally protect understandings about the evolving human condition expressed in such architecture. Thus, for example, in its enumeration of purposes, the New York City law protects access to evidence of the "noble accomplishments of the past." While the saving of architecture may also save works of beauty, the public object is less to beautify than to protect the opportunity to learn.

The preservation laws enacted in the 1960s and 1970s were an important constituent of a large, long-term shift in national attitudes, when the post-Depression, postwar American confidence in the virtues of the new—and in public action in favor of the new—began to falter. While the larger shift hinged on the failure of the war in Vietnam, the shift for buildings came when the results of the nation's enthusiastic embrace of urban renewal became vivid and permanent. The national urban policy of slum clearance was intended to address principally what buildings do. It subsidized the demolition of old buildings functionally classed as substandard so that cleared land could be sold for new buildings better adapted to new uses. When the policy failed on its own terms—when land was cleared but not redeveloped—it made wastelands of many American city centers. Even when urban renewal succeeded on the level of function, it frequently failed on the level of expression, turning the cities it benefited into placeless and disquieting downtowns of anonymous office space, highways, and parking.

Urban renewal failed as expression largely because of the shortcomings of its architectural paradigm, the semisuburban cities of towers in parks. These promising accommodations for anticipated multitudes of homogeneous, health-seeking middle-class humans presented difficulties at first unappreciated (fig. 3-2). The new buildings seemed more salubrious than the slums cleared in Europe by the bombardments of two world wars and better adapted to new

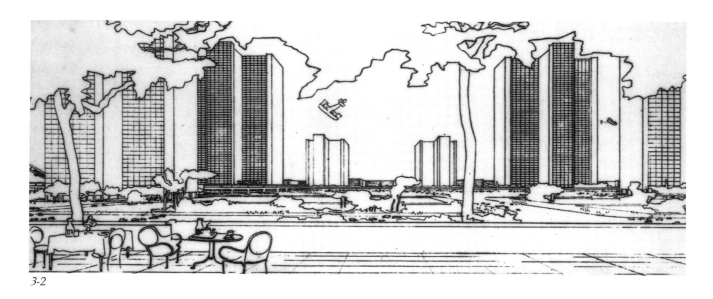

3-2

3-2. Le Corbusier's deceptively healthy paradigm for the renewal of cities

forces, still imperfectly understood, like the American willingness to sacrifice everything to the automobile. Simplified by modernist notions of form following function and the rejection of conventional ornament, the new architecture expressed admirably the meliorist nation's simplistic and obtuse near-worship of the new. In a period of growing national wealth, urban renewal placed in widely different cities buildings expressing a relatively uniform world view of a supposedly universal future human condition.

When expressed in architecture, this view of life—coupled with the shock and waste of demolition—came to seem alarming. It was hard to feel good about the prospect of life as a member of a simplified, universal, and timeless middle-class multitude. To build the context for this vision of life, renewal was destroying architecture fitted to a contrasting individualized humanity that seemed more and more attractive. Renewal was wrecking what now seemed not a dirty and outmoded past but a rich and varied continuity of individual lives. Featureless towers and windy plazas were weakening the particularity of places identified by their old architecture. It began to seem important that old buildings not be demolished. The

revived argument for the old was functional: adaptable old buildings should not be wasted. The further argument was, however, crucially expressive: old architecture should not be demolished because it is "historic," a context for real life—not in a visionary but the real world, where it would continue necessarily to be understood and lived.

The proposed definition of the term "historic" was broad: a building didn't have to be Mount Vernon to deserve protection. Candidacy for the protected class could rely on a number of factors. New York's Pennsylvania Station, the demolition of which in 1962 made preservation a forceful political movement, was the richest possible assembly of those factors. It was full of historic lessons and associations about commerce and power and civics in the United States at the end of the nineteenth century; as architecture, it was a first-class work of art; it was a rich environment in which to act out the fraction of life devoted to departure and arrival, to waiting for and catching trains; and it was literally a landmark of New York City.

This broad view connected preservation with another constituent of the great national shift in attitude toward the new: the environmental movement. Like natural environments, architecture that serves us well is important to our health. It supports our lives not just with shelter and comfort but with meaning, what it says about what we are doing, why we are doing it, and how we fit with others while we are doing it. As the source of landmarks, it gives places their identities and gives individuals their identities to the extent that they are organized around places. It also helps organize effective societies, providing monuments to focus their willingness to root for or against a home team.

Laws protecting these contributions sought not to prevent change but to regulate it. Not one tried to keep everything exactly as it was, nor did any limit itself to the prevention of demolition. Each tried to stake out and defend a range of permissible change, protecting valued architecture not like gold in a vault but as the generator of public experiences and as a source of valuable public understandings.

The laws tried to make as clear as possible in words the identity they intended to protect. This was relatively easy when a homogeneous body of valued architecture could be used as a reference, as in the solid blocks of Spanish colonial buildings of the Vieux Carré protected in New Orleans's pioneering ordinance. It was much more complex where the reference was something as heterogeneous as the existing architecture of New York City, especially because the heterogeneity itself was part of what the law was meant to protect. The need to encompass this heterogeneity was reflected in the wonderfully disjunctive list of categories covered by the New York law that meant, in the end, that anything could be protected that had a "special character." Thus, a "landmark" could be

> Any improvement, any part of which is thirty years old or older, which has a special character or special historical or aesthetic interest or value as part of the development, heritage or

cultural characteristics of the city, state or nation, and which has been designated as a landmark pursuant to the provisions of this chapter. (New York City Charter and Administrative Code, Section 25-302n.)

This breadth, of course, was unavoidable, as the object of the exercise was the protection of the city's dramatically "special" and constantly evolving "character."

Preservation laws sought to protect an identity larger than that of any particular artifact. Valued architecture was protected by a city for the city's sake, so that the protected structures would remain part of the collection of buildings that identified and benefited the city as a whole. Adding these laws, the city fit the protection of expression into its preexisting system of self-governance. The place of these new laws in the general system was made vivid in New York by the special attention given in its Landmarks Preservation Law to its relations with the city's Planning Commission and its complex zoning resolution, the product of a much earlier piece of pioneering land-use legislation. The new Landmarks Preservation Commission was expressly forbidden to make regulations about use, bulk, and height, shorthand for the business of the Planning Commission.

The point of the prohibition was only partially to avoid treading on governmental toes. Much more important, it made clear the nature of the new commission's jurisdiction. The historic business of the Planning Commission was to regulate what buildings do: their uses, the location of their uses, and the quantity of their uses, given the various municipal systems required to support them; and how the buildings housing those uses might affect the public's light and air—as, for example, in the canyons created by the Equitable Building, which had given rise to the Planning Commission in 1917. The new business of the Landmarks Commission, in contrast, was to regulate what existing buildings say, protecting valued expressions from the impact of change. Its jurisdiction to regulate expression was general. An overlay to the jurisdiction of the Planning Commission, it could also regulate use, size, and height, not in themselves but to the extent they affected expression. The laws were not in conflict. They were enacted to work together in the interest of a habitable city that would not exceed the capacity of its services, thanks to the Planning Commission, and that now, with the aid of the new Landmarks Preservation Commission, would keep its "special character."

Each city's preservation law set up a mechanism to identify the architecture it sought to protect and to judge proposals for change. To make these judgments, the laws relied on chosen representative observers, each of whom was to bring special expertise to the process, such as architectural or historical training, but to use that expertise to identify and experience valuable to anyone. The experience being protected was accessible to any interested observer—indeed, introduced at a certain level into the consciousness of every passing observer, interested or not—and protected by representative observers for the collective benefit.

The laws provided descriptions intended to help identify architecture deserving protection. In some instances the words were relatively precise, as when the protected identity could be described as having the attributes of a particular style, like Mission, and where a relatively homogeneous body of buildings corroborated the description. In the case of eclectic New York, anything could be designated that had a "special character." The limitation was that anything designated historic had to be at least thirty years old. This limitation was in part protective, so that "special" did not seem on the face of it hopelessly vague. It made a commonsense connection between history and

time, that to be preserved as historic things should be relatively old. It also recognized that the meanings of buildings are continuously changed by experience. An evolution of judgments about meaning, after all, had helped give rise to preservation laws, as the developers' International Style derivatives in renewed American cities came to seem not new and improved but appalling. Underneath the evolution was the truth about the interaction of creative work, that what follows affects what precedes, that judgments about the meanings of existing buildings evolve as they take into account the novelty, or lack of novelty, of what comes after. The thirty-year criterion served as a rough measure of the time necessary for a reasonable maturation of these judgments.

In addition to words identifying the architecture to be protected, the laws also provided their administrators standards for judging whether or not a change affecting a protected identity should be permitted. Again, where the protected work itself offered a stylistic standard, the judgment at least seemed simple to the extent that the question could be addressed as a matter of an apparent match. The underlying question, however, remained the same: that the judgment was a matter of the relationship between the old and the new. Even if a proposal seemed to match, it could never be the same, if only because of the lapse of time. The need for a judgment about the relationship would always be there.

New York's standard was expressed in a single controlling word, that new work had to be "appropriate" (New York City Charter and AdministrativeCode, Section 25-307a). The word was an important choice. It omitted any implication of sameness or matching and concentrated instead on enforcing a certain tie between conditions it expected to be different. This acknowledgment of difference reflected the nature of the city the law sought to preserve—that the protected conditions were themselves differences to be preserved—and of the phenomenon it existed to regulate, the generator of difference, change. Given the range of differences making part of the identity of New York—style, height, size, and every other architectural attribute—the range of differences permitted by the word "appropriate" was clearly very great. The word made room for the variety of "special" conditions in New York that contribute to its identity. It accommodated the vast number of possible relationships between old and new likely to be proposed in a rapidly changing city and the very large number that would necessarily fall in the acceptable range if New York were not to be made into someplace else or shut down.

The standard thus set was nevertheless restricted by the purposes of the law. To be "appropriate" a proposal had to ensure that a protected architectural expression would remain legible and effective in a particular place. The requirement permitted considerable latitude for architectural evolution and left the definition of "appropriate" to evolve decision by decision in a kind of administrative common law.

To protect expression, preservation laws set out to exercise the public's police power—its power, among other things, to prevent nuisances, the harms wrought by private activities on recognized values that the public has acquired over time the right to protect. To be able legitimately to do so, the laws had to establish that harms to protected expression were indeed harms the public was entitled to prevent. They also sought to impose their control on these harms as regulations. They sought to remain, that is, on the regulatory side of the distinction between regulations and takings. The distinction divides benefits the public can achieve by policing to prevent certain behaviors, distributing the costs of those behaviors indirectly throughout the society required to behave that way from the bene-

fits it must come up with ready cash to pay for directly, as if it had acquired them in an exercise of its right of eminent domain.

The matter ultimately is a matter of the United States Constitution and its standards for the general propriety of public restrictions on private property and for determining whether or not a particular restriction is properly considered an aspect of policing or a compensable taking. The distinction has historically been regarded in constitutional jurisprudence as a matter of degree. Thus, a requirement is considered a regulation so long as it does not "go so far as" to constitute a taking (Pennsylvania Coal Company v. Mahon et al. 260 U.S. 393, 415, 416 [1922]).

To limit their risk of crossing the line, many preservation laws simply didn't try to go very far, for example, limiting their restraint on inappropriate change to a brief period of delay before alteration could proceed. New York's law went so far as to prevent proposals for change if they could not meet the test of appropriateness or until they could meet a rigorous alternative test set out in the law for the measurement of the economic hardship imposed by the requirement of appropriateness. The choice was often simply political. The historic preservation laws of cities with an abiding sense of collective public interest, like Boston and New York, were ambitious; cities with a devotion to unfettered private enterprise, like Chicago, tended to go almost no distance at all.

Because they imposed controls on private conduct, preservation laws were contested. The most active of the contests predictably involved New York's, the most ambitious law in the most litigious city. A sequence of cases tested the designation as historic of the magnificent Greek Revival Sailors' Snug Harbor on Staten Island in New York City. The trustees of the Snug Harbor, with acres of open site available, argued that the designation unconstitutionally deprived them of their property when it forbade them to build a new high-rise sailors' home exactly in place of the old one. The New York courts rejected their argument, approving the purposes of the law and setting a standard for the lengths to which the city might constitutionally go in protecting expression: that it could police change and did not have to go through the machinery of condemnation unless the regulation "prevented or seriously interfered with" the use of the historic property for its intended purpose (In the Matter of the Trustees of the Sailors' Snug Harbor v. Platt 29 A.D. 2d 376, 377 [1968]).

The major test came in the case of Grand Central Terminal, when the Landmarks Preservation Commission found inappropriate the design of Marcel Breuer's proposed slab. The owner of the terminal, Penn Central, attacked the decision and succeeded, in the lowest court, in having it ruled unconstitutional; the trial judge decided that the old building was a long-neglected, faded beauty that didn't deserve protection. The intermediate appellate court reversed and upheld the commission's decision, noting the great value of the terminal's expression to the city's identity (Penn Central Transportation Co. et al. v. New York City et al., 50 A.D. 2d 265, 267 [1975]) and applying the established law of degree to the issue of taking. The state's highest court affirmed the intermediate court and upheld the commission's determination of inappropriateness. The matter went to the United States Supreme Court. There, in 1978, the Supreme Court confirmed that the purposes of the Landmarks law were proper purposes for the exercise of police power and that the distinction between proper regulations and improper takings was once again a matter of the degree of the restriction. On the facts of the case, the Court found that the application of the regulation left Penn Central with a valuable property and many valuable choices among ways in which it might be used or developed and therefore did not go so far as to constitute a taking (Penn Central Transportation Co. et al. v. New York City et al., 438 U.S. 104, 131 [1978]).

With general questions of propriety and power resolved at least for the moment by the Penn Central case, the principal legal matter for preservation laws remained the proper conduct of ongoing business under them, notably the satisfaction of the remaining constitutional need to apply their constraints in fair and predictable ways. These issues assumed new importance in the changing national political climate in the late 1970s and 1980s. Conceptions of the collective public interest that had at first supported preservation legislation began to yield ground to a restored sovereignty of individual property owners. Evolving standards for the identification of protected expressions and for the application of controls assumed heightened importance lest disaffected owners, frustrated in court, take action in now more sympathetic legislatures to undermine the statutes themselves. With this political anxiety, the legal interest in clarity and fairness led commissions to try various routes to predictability. New York, for example, saw a proliferation of design "guidelines" intended to describe in advance alterations that would be permitted. These guidelines risked confining all proposals within the limits of the insight and imaginations of their authors and, as precommitments, of giving away the public store.

At work was a tacit acknowledgment of the need for an accessible preservation principle both to help bring it about and to know when it had been achieved. While Penn Central and other cases had generally endorsed the regulatory activity as a whole and established that particular applications fell within the range of permissible constraints on private property, the development of a principle to inform and make arguable and predictable a succession of decisions still remained.

The New York City Landmarks Preservation Commission came closest to the development of a true body of administrative common law as it gave content to the word "appropriate" across the great volume of proposals it reviewed. When it approved or disapproved proposals as appropriate or inappropriate, it gave its reasons in writing as required by the law, calling attention to elements of form and ornament essential to the relationship of old and new.

Some of the descriptions the commission gave of proposals that did not make the grade were particularly suggestive and very important. Thus, the commission said of the Breuer design for Grand Central Terminal:

> To balance a 55-story office tower above a flamboyant Beaux-Arts facade seems nothing more than an aesthetic joke. . . . The "addition" would be four times as high as the existing structure and would reduce the landmark itself to the status of a curiosity. (New York City Landmarks Preservation Commission Decision Nos. LPC 69005, 69006.)

The words made clear that the issue was expression and, more particularly, what new architecture should or should not say about the protected architecture with which it is combined. The words described what was specifically wrong with the proposal: that it put the old building down.

In successive decisions on proposals for a large vacant site in New York's South Street Seaport Historic District, the commission made similar determinations about the way new expressions should relate to protected ones. In 1983 it rejected a simplified modernist scheme by Ulrich Franzen (fig. 3-3) in language that provided the framework for decisions on a number of subsequent appli-

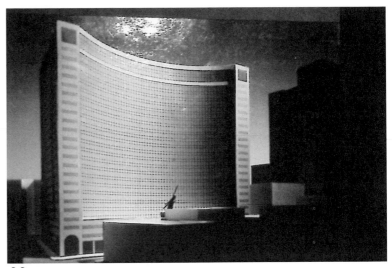

3-3

3-3. Ulrich Franzen's proposal for a new office building for the South Street Seaport Historic District in New York

3-4

3-4. Would Palmer & Hornbostel's addition have preserved H. H. Richardson's Allegheny County Courthouse in Pittsburgh, Pennsylvania?

cations. The commission saw the principal problem in the way the design handled the size of the proposed building; as designed, they said, it would "dominate and overwhelm" the protected architecture of the district. The issue was different in kind from Breuer's apparent mockery but not in principle: dominating and overwhelming the district, it also put it down. The decision went on to enumerate the sources of the expressive problems, citing "sheer" size and "boldly geom[e]tric massing," the use of "large unbroken planes . . . of a single material." The problem was in the relationship of the two expressions: the expression of the new put it at odds with the expression of the district. In its "formality and monumentality" it would be "foreign" to the district. What mattered, as in Palmer & Hornbostel's tower (fig. 3-4), was the way two expressions treated each other and, in the end, which one was honored in the combined expression.

A Test for Preservation

Focusing on these relationships, the commission acknowledged the new and the old as components of combined works that would be judged for the way they worked together. It addressed the basic issues in the evaluation of combined works—the assessment of the impacts of architecture on architecture—as it sought a rule for success that would help with the special case of preservation. It confirmed in its decisions what seems evident from a review of combined works generally, that the rule for success is somewhere in the understanding and management of relative importance, of hierarchy, in the combined expression.

In successful combined works, architects thoroughly understand and commit themselves to working with the meanings of the old buildings and contexts they have in hand, understanding being the first essential. They recognize that their new work will change the old either intentionally or inevitably, and successfully only if they change it in acceptable ways. Where they succeed, they manage the new expression so that it keeps the meaning of the old building accessible and places it in a satisfactory position in the hierarchy of the new combination.

The satisfactory position in that hierarchy varies. The old may be the background for the meaning of the combined work, like the old buildings of the Yale Art Gallery or the apartment building over the Maison de Verre. It may pervade the combined work, like the Pepsi-Cola Building at 500 Park Avenue or the Nîmes Carré d'Art. Or it may remain—indeed, be restored as—the controlling presence in the combined work, like the dome of Saint Peter's after the addition of Bernini's colonnade. The variation depends on the potential contribution of the old to the expression of the combined work, whether its inherent expressive value makes it best serve simply as contributing background or whether it is valuable and important enough that it should be allowed to dominate.

In preservation cases, this judgment of potential value and importance has effectively been made by the public act of designation. A baseline has also been established for the place the protected expression should enjoy in any future combination. By its designation, the protected identity—the meaning of the protected architecture—has been found to have special public importance and to deserve promotion at the expense of the new in the hierarchy of the combined work. The test for success in preservation is: where a public interest has attached to a building's expression, satisfactory protection of its public worth requires, first, that its meaning be accurately understood and remain understandable in any

new combination; and, second, that its meaning be respected and celebrated in the hierarchy of the combined work. Results that will satisfy the test are generally not unique but fall within a range. Success is not guaranteed by the application of any one style or approach; no rule of incongruity controls the process. But a successful result is a combined work in which the protected identity occupies the controlling role the public says it deserves.

The Protected Identity and Its Place in the New Hierarchy

Three examples illuminate the possibilities of such a test by their evident failure to meet its standard. The Lambs' Club in New York illustrates the way the identity of a building can be dissipated and lost in a new combination. The Boston Custom House vividly shows a protected identity, still present in almost all its parts, given an inappropriate role in the hierarchy of a new work. The New York Merchants' Exchange brings both points together where a vivid old building is both diluted and oppressed in a new combination. Importantly, the outcomes of the latter two projects were not disasters; to have enforced the rule against the Custom House tower or the Merchants' Exchange expansion would have deprived Boston and New York of distinguished curiosities. The point is, however, that in these combinations the originals were specifically not "preserved."

LAMBS' CLUB

McKim, Mead & White's 1906 home for the Lambs' Club in Manhattan was an attractive Georgian townhouse (fig. 3-5). Proportioned like other good works of the firm with strength and intensity in its details and

3-5

3-6

3-5. *McKim, Mead & White's original townhouse for the Lambs' Club in New York*

3-6. *George A. Freeman's inflation of the original club*

3-7. *The Lambs' Club today*

3-7

organization, it was not a great building but a satisfactory architectural expression that might have been worthy of public protection given that satisfactory buildings are rarer than they should be.

When George Freeman doubled the size of the club in 1912, he did not simply to add to it: he inflated it sideways (fig. 3-6). The original resolute up-and-down rectangle became an irresolute square. The set-back attic was brought forward so that the principal plane of the façade ran uninterrupted into the sky. This eliminated the transition important to the façade's hierarchy, one that had established its proportions and closed the composition at the top. The coigns at the western edge of the original were moved to the new western edge, twice as far from their eastern counterparts and, as a result, roughly half as intense in their relationship across twice as much brick. On the inflated plane the ordered windows, pilasters, and other elements of the original were doubled, losing impact as individuals and as energetic participants in their relationships. Diluted by duplication, their meanings became unclear; there were now, for example, two front doors and no way to know which was the front door or whether either one really was an effective entry into the building.

New details were added in an effort to sort things out, like the decorative plaque at the intersection of the diagonals of the new façade under the swag that had centered the townhouse. These emphasized by their lack of distinction and unclear purpose what had happened: the strength and identity of the façade had been drained away. The diffused bits and weakened idea left the Lambs' a souvenir of itself. However pervasive the reminders, from the point of view of preservation—the protection and celebration of a valued identity— the thing itself was pretty much gone (fig. 3-7).

3-8

UNITED STATES CUSTOM HOUSE

If the expansion of the Lambs' Club dissipated the identity for which one might have
wanted to preserve it, something interestingly different but equally difficult happened to Ammi Young's 1837 Boston Custom House (fig. 3-8) when it found itself,
like the cartographer's tortoise, having to
bear up Peabody and Stearns's 1915 expansion (fig. 3-9).

When it was erected, the Custom House
symbolized the importance to the United
States of customs duties, then the nation's
most important source of revenues. The
modified Greek temple was a huge public
investment. A stocky, domed landmark of
great density immediately on the waterfront, it received and kept its users' offer-
ings like a strongbox. It apparently per-
formed more or less as intended until, in a
feat of ingenious and costly wartime alteration, the very tall and slender campanile
of offices was superimposed squarely on its
shoulders. Space was found for elevators
and stairs in the thick masonry corners of
the old building. Virtually the entire Custom House stayed in place, including not
only its dome—now buried in the shaft—

3-9

*3-8. Ammi Young's 1837 strongbox
for the United States Custom House in
Boston*

*3-9. The Custom House under
Peabody & Stearns's tower*

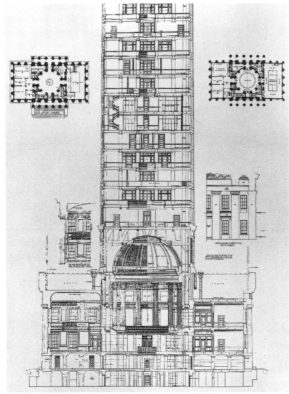

3-10

3-11

3-10. Peabody & Stearns's provisions for the preservation of the Custom House in the alteration

3-11. The Custom House still bearing up

but even the possibility of air and borrowed light continuing to enter through the oculus of the dome, given the openings provided on all four sides of the square tower that engulfed it (fig. 3-10).

The expansion kept the Custom House in use and permitted it once again to participate as a landmark in a taller Boston. But while the expansion maintained its physical identity in an ingenious new building, the reality was nonetheless very uncomfortable and compromising for the old building in itself. Its head lost in the tall Venetian tower, the old building had been delivered up bound and blind to the support of the new (fig. 3-11). In its literal and figurative subordination in a combination celebrating the new, it was hard to say that the Custom House itself had been preserved.

NEW YORK MERCHANTS' EXCHANGE

McKim, Mead & White's expansion of Isaiah Rogers's New York Merchants' Exchange likewise seems not to have preserved it.

The long colonnade and central gilt dome of Rogers's truncated and slightly skewed version of Karl Friedrich Schinkel's Altes Museum (fig. 3-12) was an important presence on Wall Street from its construction in 1842 until the end of the century. With its own intensity and its evocative connection to Schinkel and German romanticism (fig. 3-13), it introduced above the still low fabric of the city the more adventurous post-Republican American architecture that would take off with the Gothic Revival at Trinity Church a few years later. After service as New York's Custom House and various intermediate physical tinkerings, including the addition of an attic story (fig. 3-14), the building was bought by the First National City Bank and committed to McKim, Mead & White for expansion as the bank's headquarters.

**NEW YORK MERCHANTS'
EXCHANGE**
New York, New York

*Isaiah Rogers, 1842
McKim, Mead & White, 1910*

*3-12. Isaiah Rogers's original New
York Merchants' Exchange on Wall
Street in New York*

*3-13. Rogers's source, Schinkel's Altes
Museum, Berlin, today*

*3-14. The Merchants' Exchange
in use as a Custom House*

3-12

3-14

3-13

3-15

3-16

3-15. The Merchants' Exchange about to be absorbed by the First National City Bank

3-16. The Merchants' Exchange today

In 1909 the firm boldly doubled the building and its colonnade, superimposing on Rogers's Ionic columns a second set distinguished almost exclusively by their Corinthian capitals. The dome was absorbed into the new mass, becoming a central feature of the new banking floor. The whole was apparently supposed to be part of a still larger composition involving a tall building behind the banking floor, but the last part was not built. The surviving double colonnade is still one of the most important façades on Wall Street (figs. 3-15 and 3-16).

The doubling and superimposition of the colonnade had simultaneously the effects of the expansion of the Lambs' Club and the superimposition of the Boston Custom House tower. While the repetition of the original columns kept the expanded Exchange familiar, the doubled number diluted them virtually to anonymity. With nothing to distinguish them, Rogers's columns lost their novelty. Most important, in the new stacked organization they changed character. As in the Schinkel façade they imitated, their handsome, repeated presences said more about order, rhythm, and proportion—about the romantic drama of a long low run like Schinkel's— than about holding things up. Now both the old building and its columns were put to work in a vertical system that was chiefly about weight, stability, and support—banking, perhaps, rather than commerce—and they were the bottom of the system.

While reminders of the Altes Museum remain in the block of the building and the way its ends hold the new double colonnade, the change of character undid the connection Rogers made with the definitive feature of the most important building of his time. An observer can still figure out what is going on but this requires knowledge and an exercise of memory to undo what was done by the addition. The original no longer calls out in the combination as something important offering lessons to be learned but is absorbed and changed like raw material. Once the original is made out, what is most impressive is the curiosity of its position in the new composition, the obvious labor imposed on it as the bearer of the addition. Like Young's Custom House in Boston, Rogers's exterior physically survived, but what it intended to say as a work of art it could only say as if with considerable effort and through gritted teeth.

These three combinations, however interesting, seem unsatisfactory as "preservation." An original expression protected for its public worth should not have to be puzzled out of supervening architecture. It should remain free to convey its valued meanings for the public benefit, not in spite of the new combination but with its support, as the honored and controlling part of the combined work.

The test suggested by this understanding of preservation is borne out when it is applied to a longer series of cases and controversies where preservation was expressly an issue, where public interest had been asserted in an original work, and where public opinion or an actual application of law was asserted to protect it. The test helps make clear what went wrong and what might have been done to make it come out right.

Securing the Place of the Protected Identity

The first part of the test is its requirement that the protected meaning be accurately understood and remain understandable in any new combination. Cases focusing on this part suggest ways the understanding of meaning can help sort out arguments about its protection. Here meaning plays the role of reason in the old maxim *cessante ratione,*

cessat ipsa lex—the reason for the expression (its meaning)—helps determine what portions of the expression must survive and what need not.

The first case involves the removal of a 1920s addition to New York's Central Park, a work of art with a particularly strong identity and an equally long and loud history of political conflict about whether and how that identity should be recognized and protected. The second involves a proposal for an interesting new work of art—James Stirling's design for Number One Poultry Lane in London—whose gestation and delivery as a contributor to the city might have been eased by a better understanding of its context.

NAUMBERG BANDSHELL, CENTRAL PARK

Administrators of Olmstead and Vaux's 1860s masterwork, Central Park, proposed to remove a later addition, the 1920s Naumberg Bandshell, as part of a major park renovation. They lost in a replay of a political conflict that has dogged the park since its construction: whether the park is somehow for one group of New Yorkers rather than another. In conflict were two not very helpful views of the identity to be protected. What was at stake was either an old work of art—a position tarred as elitist—or an artifact composed of the original park and the subsequent accretions that gave witness, among other things, to the ongoing political struggle about the true beneficiaries of the park—a position held up as democratic. The conflict was resolved by a deus ex machina, an old and silly statute that apparently forbids the City of New York ever to disembarrass itself of gifts. This resolution ironically protected the position of the democrats by protecting one particular piece of "elitism," the patronage of the Naumbergs who gave the bandshell to the city. At the same time it perpetuated a con-

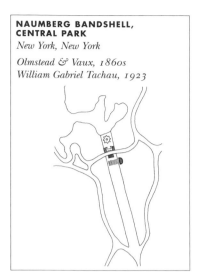

3-17. *Olmstead and Vaux's Central Park: a health-giving public work*

3-18. *The reward of the Park's inducement to movement*

3-17

3-18

flict between the park and one of its subsequent improvements that might have been easier to resolve if the meaning of the protected original had been better understood.

The conflict had to do with the design of the park as a health-giving public work and the impact on that design of a device, ostensibly serving the same purpose, that in fact undermines it. Conceived as the successor to the Croton Aqueduct and intended to do with fresh air what the aqueduct did with water, Central Park organizes its vast acres around systems of curving paths and roads dotted with prospects and architectural devices to reward and spur movement in the open air, inducements to New Yorkers to get out of doors and breathe (fig. 3-17). At the end of all the paths, topping the park's formal hierarchy, is the Mall and the climactic straight-line progress it organizes to the ornamental steps of the Bethesda Terrace and down to the revelation of the Bethesda Fountain and the Angel of the Waters, the park's focal celebration of the healing qualities of water and fresh air (fig. 3-18). There, with a woman's body, by a woman sculptor—firsts for their time—the Angel winds into the celebration an homage to a contemporary view of women as angelic players of a similar healing role.

Central Park had a bandstand from the beginning—the light, ornate hexagonal Music Stand designed by the architect of the park's finest features, Jacob Wrey Mould. Like other bandstands, Mould's Music Stand (fig. 3-19) was intended as an attraction, using music to draw people to and engage them in important events. Like other bandstands, it dispensed music as an incident and an inducement to movement, not as a static opportunity to concentrate on works of musical art. The Music Stand put its music at the entry to the terrace and the head of the steps down

3-19

3-20

3-21

3-19. Jacob Mould's Music Stand: music as part of the inducement

3-20. At first music is central at the top of the climactic steps

3-21. Later, music encourages the descent from the side

93

3-22

3-23

3-22. *The Naumberg Bandshell fixes
its listeners in place*

3-23. *The dog in the manger today*

to the Bethesda Fountain, right at the top of the Mall's progress toward the biggest event in the park. First from the middle (fig. 3-20) and then from the side, it drew users to the climax of the design, supporting and intensifying their movement toward it (fig. 3-21).

The original bandstand and its music were extremely popular, but no more resistant to wear and tear than any other part of the park's architecture. The 1920s Naumberg proposal was the last of a succession of designs to replace it as it crumbled away. These grew larger and larger and took an increasingly formal and serious view of music not as incidental to movement but as something improving that one should sit down and listen to. With obvious willingness to impose improvement on park users, the Naumberg Bandshell asked listeners to sit still in rows and to focus their attention on an axial, classical half-shell dispenser of sound. This different expectation with respect to music and behavior was made more imposing by the bandshell's form—its unshadowed white Columbian Exposition formality—and by its location; the rows of immobile if relaxed music-lovers were set at ninety degrees to the axis of the Mall, cutting across it just before the terrace and the stairs (fig. 3-22). Not only did it cut across the progress of the Mall but it established an event at the top of the stair competing with the terrace and the Angel. At the top of the hierarchy of the park, it stuck like a bone in the throat.

The Naumberg Bandshell served the increasing number of people free to use the park in the Depression and in the decades thereafter, offering them opportunities to focus on music, or on dance associated with music, in the concentrated way its architecture required. In the 1960s, a period of social change and gross neglect of the park, the architectural confusion created by the self-important focus of the bandshell, together with the crumbling asphalt required for its seating, contributed materially to the decline of the terrace.

In the 1970s and 1980s, serious interest in the park revived. The bandshell and the events it served declined as popular draws, replaced by looser, larger gatherings in the park's great open spaces. Attention refocused on the park as a venue for such popular gatherings and—most happily, given its original intention—for outdoor exercise in the form of running, walking, and other forms of movement. At the top of the stair the pavement in front of the bandshell became a favored place for happy, sweaty skate dancers who stood or moved around the music of boom boxes the way their perspiring ancestors had moved around the original bandstand.

As part of a comprehensive restoration of the values of the park's original design, its administrators proposed that the big, dilapidated Naumberg Bandshell be removed. They called attention to its bad condition and to the conflict of its Columbian Exposition white classicism with the much more delicate original features of the park. The functional conflict was not addressed except by implication in the proposal that the Bandshell be reinstalled elsewhere, a reasonable proposition given that its virtues as a classical artifact and as a distributor of music to a public seated in rows did not have to be in Central Park to be appreciated. The corollary of the proposal—the compromise of the Park as a work of art, as it could not fully do its business with the bandshell stuck in its throat—was not explicitly argued. The matter was left as a somewhat superficial balancing of amenities—how much prettier the park would be relandscaped and without the shell—with the deeper and possibly more helpful understanding of the conflict unexplored.

When New York's peculiar law about gifts froze the conflict in place, it preserved an anomaly of some interest, evidence of the many conflicts that have marked the park's use and stewardship, of the differences among its users over time and the different sorts of outdoor improvement they imposed on the park's original system. The bandshell had a claim to protection as an artifact, being mentioned in the park's designation report, but its status as an anomaly—its conflict with the meaning of the park—was not called out or specifically protected. Given the notion that the protected work should control the outcome of subsequent architectural work and assuming this understanding of the park and the place of music in it, the conflict seems relatively easy to resolve. In any event, the guardians of the protected park, the Landmarks Preservation Commission, did not see the anomaly as having the worth of its piece of landscape and thought the bandshell should go. As things stand, the conflict is still there, mitigated by revised landscaping. The bandshell represents its era on the Mall and looks better for a coat of paint. But it remains for all that a big white dog in the manger, its muted bark still distracting from the progress of the Mall to the Angel of the Waters, its uptight and inflexible shell still protesting the renewed athletic movement of a popular and serviceable old public work (fig. 3-23).

NUMBER ONE POULTRY LANE

For James Stirling's ambitious design for Number One Poultry Lane, a triangular block at a crucial intersection in the City of London (fig. 3-24), a better understanding of the thing to be preserved might have helped resolve more than thirty years of conflict.

The buildings to be replaced, relatively straightforward Victorian offices by John Belcher (fig. 3-25), were surrounded by institutions of an entirely different order of importance. Face to face was the Bank of

3-24

3-25

3-24. James Stirling's proposal
for One Poultry Lane

3-25. The Victorian occupants
of the site

England, a majestic work of Sir John Soane. Across the street was James Lutyens's magnificent Midland Bank. Adjacent were the Mansion House and Hawksmoor's Saint Mary Woolnoth. Together at this extraordinary intersection, the buildings were the "Heart of the Empire," muscular instruments of the institutions that bound together the great global British achievement (fig. 3-26). The demolition of the Victorian buildings would change the context, but would it change its meaning?

The proposal for Poultry Lane had an architectural history of its own. The developer first invited Mies van der Rohe to design what would have been his first building in London, a metal and glass tower in the International Style that would have been at home in any of the world's post–World War II financial centers (fig. 3-27). However appropriate for its time, it might have diluted the peculiar identity of the Heart of the Empire with an important element neither imperial nor British nor otherwise identified with London, a factor that may have contributed to its rejection by the guardians of London's character.

The developer got a very different expressive response from the next architect, James Stirling. Where Mies would have devoted part of the block to a plaza—a commonplace of International-Style urbanism that came to be much loathed—Stirling's building reoccupied the whole triangular block, filling it out to the street like the buildings it replaced and like the other buildings that generate the City's characteristic dense and crooked urban form. Stirling then molded and modeled on the triangle an animated restatement of the old building with an amplified winged tower at its apex (fig. 3-28), a sympathetic contemporary expression of the eccentric, plastic identity established for London by Wren and Hawksmoor after the Great Fire of 1666. He shaped the new triangular baroque mass around a very large, per-

96

3-26

3-27

3-28

3-26. The site as Heart of the Empire

3-27. Mies van der Rohe's proposed
International Style office block and
plaza

3-28. Stirling's much more
baroque design

3-29. Number One
Poultry Lane as built

fectly circular interior atrium, a favorite
organizing device that in this case served as
an emblem, in its pure geometry, of the uni-
versality of its city's imperial ambitions and
its sometime power over the world.

Stirling's building survived extended con-
troversy and was finished in 1997 (fig. 3-29).
Standing up to the immediate and powerful
challenge of his predecessors and architectural neighbors, Stirling contributed a major
new element to the larger identity of the City
of London that restates in a complex and
interesting way the special meaning of its
unusual urban intersection. Wedged powerfully into its site, Number One Poultry Lane
does something the Victorian buildings did
not do on behalf of a London much more
richly understood and still alive.

Assuming the identity to be protected is correctly identified and understood, preservation then requires that the protected meaning be respected and celebrated in the hierarchy of the new combined work, remaining
in control of the new combination. A major
proposal to expand Louis Kahn's Kimbell
Museum can illustrate how subtle and difficult it can be to draw the line when the proposal is a very close adaptation that expands
on some of the wonders of a great original
but possibly compromises others. Where the
proposal actually imitates the original, two
examples suggest the range of possibilities.
At one end, the work of Quinlan Terry
shows the risks of pastiche; at the other, the
Dana Center in Central Park illustrates legitimate uses of imitation.

KIMBELL ART MUSEUM

Facing pressures to accommodate large works and traveling shows, the Kimbell Museum in Fort Worth, Texas, asked Romaldo Giurgola in 1989 to see if he could extend the treasure house Louis Kahn completed for the museum in 1972 (fig. 3-30). To do so Giurgola proposed to adapt and expand upon an implication of the master's design, the apparent modular nature of its vaults (fig. 3-31), multiplying the extraordinary slotted pairs of beams that form the long silvery cassones holding the museum's exceptionally fine works of art (fig. 3-32). In the new groups of

KIMBELL ART MUSEUM
Fort Worth, Texas

Louis I. Kahn, 1972
Mitchell/Giurgola Associates, 1989

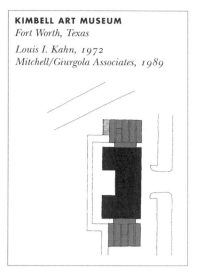

3-30. Aerial view of Louis Kahn's warehouse for the treasures of the Kimbell Art Museum

3-31. The approach to the original group of vaults

3-32. Inside the vaults

3-30

3-31

3-32

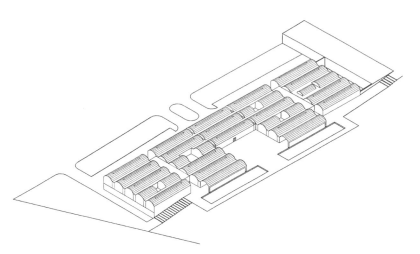

3-33

3-34

3-33. Romaldo Giurgola's proposed extension

3-34. A reconstruction of the Porticus Aemilia from 1965

vaults he attached at both ends of the original sets (fig. 3-33) Giurgola repeated Kahn's alignment of the vaults side to side and end to end. With the exception of a slightly enlarged joint to call out the new groups from the old, he gave the spaces between the vaults similar sizes and uses. He then extended the pattern of courts Kahn cut through his carpet of vaults to tie the whole together, adding courts of appropriate sizes and placement in the extensions. The multiplication of the vaults exploited an implication of the vaulted Roman storehouse that might have been in Kahn's mind, the Porticus Aemilia (fig. 3-34): in theory, the parallel storage vaults could be happily multiplied forever.

While he was making out of the old what clearly promised to be more of a very good thing, Giurgola distinguished his new formal units from the old. For example, he opened up the ends of his vaults to a greater degree than Kahn had opened the originals and he changed the diffuser for light coming through the famous slot. He separated the new vaults into two subgroups serving the original group between them. The gaps between the original and the new groups were greater than the gaps between the vaults of the original museum. These wider gaps had new functions as subordinate entries and circulation spaces on either side of the original museum and served as distinct spatial events marking the lateral passage from the old into the new.

Giurgola did not repeat in front of the new groups the special open vaults that flank the original entry. Kahn's abstracted revelations of the essential elements of the museum's architecture—the bones of his cassones and the immediate marvel of their unsupported length—belong exclusively to the original entry and museum; they are part of the initial experience by which visitors are introduced and drawn into the Museum from each of its lateral approaches (fig. 3-35). Without the open introductory vault and with five vaults rather than the six of the adjacent original, the new groups are automatically set back from the plane of the original museum and are clearly subordinate to it.

Emphasizing the modularity of the vaults as a way to change and expand the museum, Giurgola's proposal necessarily downplayed a crucial, conflicting aspect of Kahn's design, the limitation of its size. Kahn's Kimbell was intentionally small, reduced step by step in the course of its design to represent and hold a limited and virtually unchanging collection of works of the highest quality, as does New York's Frick Collection. His assembly of vaults fits precisely on top of his underlying box of servant spaces, the perfectly flat side walls shown off by voids on three sides, with the box and the ends of the vaults sheared off to match their planes exactly. Kahn's intended side approaches to the Kimbell make the sense of limitation in these walls an inescapable part of the initial impression of the museum; it begins and ends exactly at these sides. Pushed out by Giurgola's addition, the tightness of the original limitation—the almost painful slicing off of the sides at the planes of the entries (fig. 3-36)— and the density and intensity of the form as a whole, might not have been as striking. The crucial introductory porticos would no longer begin exactly where the museum did but rather, after a relaxed interval, at a point one vault back from the beginning.

This loss of emphasis on limitation would have been compounded by a similar loss from the proposed increase in the number of vaults. If additional vaults were not sufficiently different from Kahn's, the loss of distinction would deprive the latter of the value of their originality. If the vaults in fact became modules, they would be theoretically innumerable, the opposite of the notion of the limited container. More importantly, perhaps, the increase in number would undermine the sense of scarcity—that there are only so many vaults—that supports and

3-35

3-36

3-35. One of Kahn's introductory porticos

3-36. The sliced-off end at the limit of the original

**DOWNING COLLEGE:
THE MAITLAND ROBINSON
LIBRARY**

Cambridge, England

*William Wilkins, 1806
Herbert Baker et al., 1920, 1950
Quinlan Terry, 1994*

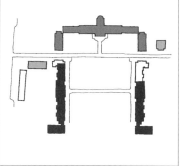

3-37. Incomplete after a century's building, Downing College at Cambridge University looks like Thomas Jefferson's University of Virginia

3-38. Wilkins's original façade would have closed the end and made his pieces most important

3-39. One side of the original range

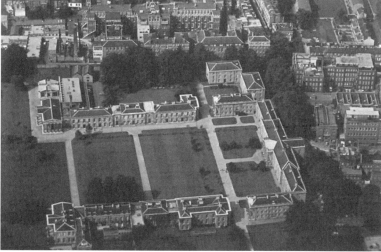

3-37

3-38

3-39

enriches the effects of their silvery light and the wonder of their unsupported length.

Giurgola and the museum put forward the proposal for serious consideration and ran into serious criticism. Its alteration of the balance between modularity and limitation seemed to compromise a composition felt to be just right as it was. The various distinctions proposed between old and new were seen as insufficient to preclude the risk of diluting the old. The increase in the size of the museum overall was seen as overrunning the limitation Kahn so carefully expressed, substituting a looser, less intense composition. In a context in which it was possible to doubt the added value generally—museum expansions were growing more controversial—and given the risks to the institution in the public perception that it was taking a risk with a masterpiece, the museum abandoned its experiment with this route to growth.

DOWNING COLLEGE:
THE MAITLAND ROBINSON LIBRARY

The problems of Giurgola's proposed close adaptation of the Kimbell introduce those of more direct imitations. The first is dilution of the identity of the old, where it is hard to tell where the old ends and the new begins. The second is competition with the old; it can be hard to tell which is being celebrated—the original inventive achievement or something that seeks the benefit of its success like a parasite. The closer the imitation, it is fair to say, the greater the problem.

The problem takes acute form in new works that purport literally to continue old styles. These are often offered as part of a polemic about the evils of modernity, arguing that we were somehow better in the past and will be better now if we go on as if nothing has happened. Somewhat more subtly, the argument is that, if not better, we are at least the same, even if we have traded in our stock and breeches for the occasional coat and tie, and can properly represent some unchanging essence of ourselves in old architectural idioms—as if we still said "Zwounds" and "Gadzooks." Works relying on this argument offer the naïve and unsuspecting the apparent comfort of an architecture they think they like, as well as a pretense of continuity and a polemical claim of legitimacy. Like other forms of theming, the hyperreality of these technical simulations competes with and obscures the real and makes its lessons still harder to appreciate.

Additions designed by Quinlan Terry at Downing College, one of Cambridge University's most interesting college complexes, show the implications of this polemic and its architecture. The architecture of Downing College began in an early-nineteenth-century competition won by William Wilkins. Wilkins proposed a long sequence of plain Greek classical pavilions wrapped around a large rectangular lawn that now seems to anticipate Jefferson by some years (fig. 3-37), though this lawn was meant to be closed (fig. 3-38). Wilkins was able to build only a portion of his design (fig. 3-39), some of the side dormitory blocks and two beautifully porticoed corner pieces that frame the open end of the lawn and are the high points of the original composition (fig. 3-40). The rest was built in increments over more than a century, all of them, remarkably, in a related plain, classical style. The effort to accommodate within a classical style the vast changes of more than a century culminated in the elegant curiosity of Sir Herbert Baker's twin Ionic pavilions in 1932 at the corners opposite Wilkins's, absorbing with some grace three stories in a form intended by Wilkins only for two (fig. 3-41). The continuation of the style even into the late 1960s for the long range of buildings across the end of the lawn can be understood as architectural self-effacement, the new buildings like plain clay used in a museum reconstruction to show

3-40

3-41

3-42

3-40. An original piece built by Wilkins in 1810

3-41. A three-story interpretation of Wilkins from the 1930s

3-42. Terry's interpretation: the Maitland Robinson Library

*3-43. The Dana Center
in Central Park*

off Wilkins's antique fragments in a semblance of their original vase.

Protecting the importance of Wilkins's fragments is difficult because they are parts of an incomplete design that lacks the support of the relatively elaborate centerpiece with which he planned to close and contain the lawn. The entries to the college come in laterally at the opposite end of the lawn from Wilkins's buildings, along an avenue that enters the quadrangle near its newest corners and reveals a romantic vista so compelling that it is hard to remember to look for Wilkins's architecture. In the 1990s Quinlan Terry compounded the problem of distraction by adding, outside the entry corners, eye-catching classical theme pavilions of aggressive self-importance. On one side is a yellow box for a theater, roughly the size of the old buildings but more vertical, dressed with great care in trappings of a Restoration architecture that seems foppish. On the other side, at the principal entry to the college, is the Maitland Robinson Library, a tour de force of resurrected Doric (fig. 3-42).

Terry's buildings have the problems of their twentieth-century classical predecessors in accommodating change. Modern lighting, for example, shows incongruously through the windows, revealing them as the thickest of veneers. More serious in Terry's buildings is their self-absorbed elaboration and the noisy pretense of correctness that makes inescapable their misunderstanding of the buildings around them as a polemic, not a work of art. Wilkins may have had a broad faith in classicism. What he left at Downing was a beautiful and original application of early-nineteenth-century classicism to the design of a particular collegiate institution. In their attentuated simplicity Wilkins's buildings call on subsequent masters, in Goethe's prescription, for restraint. Instead, the oblivious Terry puts down the Maitland Robinson like a classical boom box and turns it on.

3-43

DANA CENTER, CENTRAL PARK

The Dana Center in Olmstead and Vaux's Central Park imitates the old style in a different way and in the service of a different work of art. An addition to the system of health-giving recreational movement set up in the original park design, the center is the latest of the pavilions intended to attract and reward walkers of the park's paths—in this case, walkers to the remote northeast corner of the park and the outside edge of one of its largest and formerly most neglected water features, the Harlem Meer (fig. 3-43). The center adopts the spiky polychrome architecture of the first park buildings with porches, porticoes, a steeply pitched and pinnacled tile roof, and rich, multicolored ornamentation.

The center stands not only at the extremity of the park but also at a wide, low point north of some of its highest and most historic rocky heights, where the park tends to leak away into the surrounding city. The new building is sized to be not too big for its adopted idiom but at the same time an effective presence and marker for one of the defining corners of the park. In this position Buttrick White & Burtis's imitation makes the connection with the old park downtown, reestablishing for the neglected corner and its neighborhood the benefit of association with a prestigious work of art and extending the identity of the original park. The new building itself benefits from the association in a way that serves the purposes of the whole, not just its own.

Protecting Particular Sources of Identity

The principal meanings of protected works are generated by different parts of their anatomy. In some, for example, it is the form that does the work; in others it is the plan. Additions most affect protected works when they alter the parts most important to their meaning.

Façades and Façadomy

Façades are buildings' single most obvious source of meaning, often clearly applied for the purpose. Like that slid onto the Cambridge Old Schools by Stephen Wright in 1758 to make it a better neighbor for the Senate House (see fig. 3-1), these façades have a degree of independence from the buildings behind them and are often replacements stuck on to update meaning. Façades with this degree of detachment can actually be portable: when endangered, they can be cut off and displayed elsewhere, in a museum or on another building. The results of façadomy—the degree to which slicing off and rehanging constitutes preservation—have less to do with the pleasures of contemplating designs that transportation can preserve than with the further value that comes from maintaining the designs in place and the meanings that are necessarily lost when they are taken elsewhere.

Architectural expression constructs its meanings in particular physical contexts and under the aesthetic, moral, and practical assumptions of particular times. Given its immobility and durability, architecture frequently continues to assert those meanings in those places long after the contexts and assumptions have changed. The illuminating incongruities that result are among the chief values protected by preservation and among those lost when façades are moved.

SECOND BRANCH BANK OF THE UNITED STATES
New York, New York

Martin Thompson, 1824

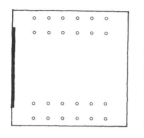

3-44. Martin Thompson's Branch Bank design

3-45. The Branch Bank as the Assay Office, on Wall Street

3-46. The façade in 1914 just before it was removed

3-47. The façade applied to the Metropolitan Museum

3-48. The façade on exhibit in the Metropolitan

SECOND BRANCH BANK OF THE UNITED STATES

The Second Branch Bank of the United States in New York City, part of the early and controversial initiative of the federal government to exploit its responsibility for the federal "fisc," was designed by Martin Thompson and built on Wall Street in 1824 next to old Federal Hall, the building that had housed the United States government for the year New York was the nation's first capital (fig. 3-44). Through the bank, the branch was connected with its inventor, the New Yorker Alexander Hamilton, and the exceedingly important deal he worked out in a neighboring tavern during the first session of Congress. In his deal, the infant federal government assumed the debts of the states, gaining a huge measure of authority over them. In exchange, to be more closely under the watchful gaze of Virginia and the agricultural South, the seat of government was moved from New York to the swamp that became the District of Columbia.

The façade of the branch displayed the enduring and pervasive interest of its architect and of its time in classical Greek and Roman precedents for the architecture of the young Republic. Clearly a surface applied for representational purposes in order to make associations with a particular set of values, the handsome, unpretentious, local-marble façade came shortly to contrast with the much more ambitious three-dimensional development of the same ideas in the Doric temple built by the United States next door. When President Andrew Jackson put the bank out of business in a burst of anti-elitism, the Branch became the federal assay office (fig. 3-45). When the assay office yielded to commercial development in 1915 (fig. 3-46), the façade was given to the Metropolitan Museum (fig. 3-47). It now hangs as an object on the south face of the Ameri-

3-44

3-45

106

can Wing, addressing and supporting the other artworks in the Engelhart Courtyard (fig. 3-48).

Applied to the wall of the American Wing, Martin Thompson's façade still distributes much pleasure as a representative and successful classical composition. It still faces south as it did on Wall Street and, because of the glazing of the court, is still modulated by the changing light and shadow of day. The omission of the protective grilles on the ground-floor windows and the way its front door gives onto a gallery of domestic furnishings weakens its specific connection with banking. The meaning it has as a piece of the history of the United States is scarcely added back by the available labels.

What Thompson's façade cannot do from its place on the Metropolitan's wall is call out on Wall Street the parts of its meaning that are critical to the understanding of that peculiarly important, and peculiarly New York, place. The overwhelming power of the street and its multiple incongruities often make its riches of meaning hard to appreciate. Left in place, the little representative of the Bank of the United States would have helped link the incongruities to their sources in national history. The size and style of the façade said something immediate and important about the growth of the Republic and the enormous inflation with it of the great financial institutions still functioning on Wall Street. It further made evident the rapidity of that inflation in its obvious contrast with the much bigger, stronger temple placed next to it only eight years later. Representing the Bank of the United States, it made a direct connection with the crucial early months of the United States and the moment New York City surrendered the federal capital and tightened its bonds with Mammon. In its almost incomprehensible difference in size, it heightened the drama of the street's display of what followed from the choices.

3-46

3-47

3-48

3-49

3-50

3-49. The façade of the Pennsylvania
Fire Insurance Company

3-50. Mitchell/Giurgola's model with
the old façade, the intermediate
expansions, and the new tower

PENN MUTUAL LIFE INSURANCE COMPANY

The façade of the Second Branch might in fact have stayed in place, given the right kind of architectural imagination. The kind of help it would have needed—and what it might have been able to contribute had it got that help— is well illustrated by Romaldo Giurgola's reuse of the façade of the Penn Mutual Life Insurance Company in the company's expanded headquarters in Philadelphia.

The façade he used was originally the façade of a 22-foot-wide, three-bay, four-story Egyptian Revival building designed by John Haviland for the Pennsylvania Fire Insurance Company, expanded to six bays by T. P. Chandler in 1902 (fig. 3-49). Its Egyptian references held interesting associations for an insurance company with time and timelessness, as well as with the occult and notions of what happens to policyholders after the event that allows the beneficiaries of their life insurance policies to collect. The doubled building then stood adjacent to two further expansions by Edgar V. Seeler and Ernest J. Matthewson, which took over the block all the way to the corner and by 1931 filled it with twenty stories of granite.

To expand the headquarters yet again in the 1960s, Giurgola proposed to replace the building behind the old façade with a tower rising up beside the great gray bulk of the last expansions (fig. 3-50). He retained the old façade as a screen at the foot of the new tower, still attached to the row of townhouses of which it had always been part. There, after a gap for the entry to the new tower, it remained the point of reference for the two entry pavilions that the pre-1931 expansions derived from the old building as devices to settle themselves into the street and relate to the beginnings of the company.

Like his immediate predecessors, Giurgola used the old façade to give scale to his tower and tie it into place and to the ground, but he did so as a convinced modernist in a way that exploited the potential of its abstraction as an applied façade (fig. 3-51). The façade remained attached to the old row of houses but differed from them and was abstracted from them because there now was no house behind it. Instead, a concrete supporting frame was attached to make the old façade freestanding—a compression and abstraction of the old structure. The dark, recessed entry to the new tower was around the façade, not through it, and its windows were removed. The façade's functions as entry and as enclosure were thus cut away (fig. 3-52).

This abstraction eliminated functions the façade clearly could no longer sensibly perform and at the same time brought out the much more important value of its expression. Set in the dark glass recess made in the tower to receive it, its white, reflective stone and old systems of proportion and decoration stood out in their relative intensity and familiarity from the large, unadorned planes of glass and concrete of the modern tower. Above the recess the balance of the new shaft was organized by lines from the old façade, like traces of its impact. On the sides of the tower detached screens of square openings shaded the curtain wall— the screen of the old façade, still more abstracted, making its influence felt in a modern application. In the recess the façade remained vivid as the source and anchor for the three-part combined work organized around it. There the façade that had identified Penn Mutual from the beginning played the role it had always been intended to play as a graphic (fig. 3-53). It marked by the contrasts of its abstraction and size the extraordinary growth and change in the company, in architecture, and in the world in the intervening years.

The Penn Mutual building is now more or less abandoned by its company. The concrete of the tower has aged yellow, stained, rough,

3-51

3-52

3-53

3-51. *The façade still in place on the street*

3-52. *The abstracted façade on its frame at the entry*

3-53. *The façade and the screen wall derived from it on the street side*

109

and ugly against the adjacent stone. Most sadly, the row of buildings of which the façade was part has been demolished. Now the composition begins not with the real but with the first abstraction. The façade is still where it should be but without the neighbors that helped make clear the continuity it provided.

Plans

Alterations at the University of Virginia and the Salk Institute reworked plans that were the heart of the identity of each work of art. At the University of Virginia, the remarkable original plan was deliberately suppressed by a university bent on changing character with its times. At the Salk Institute, the original plan seems not to have been adequately understood by the succeeding architect and the owner, even though both made much of their intimate knowledge of and affection for the original architect and his design.

UNIVERSITY OF VIRGINIA

Jefferson's academical village was an astonishing mechanism invented by him to fit higher education to the specific circumstances of the young Republic (fig. 3-54). Designed with significant help from Benjamin Latrobe, the invention, like the nation, took the West as its object, addressing the national frontier in the distance beyond the mountains (fig. 3-55). Like the nation at the time, it was completely open-ended and willingly exposed to the unknown (fig. 3-56). It was entered at the bottom, its open end, from a rural lane by a deliberately rustic wooden gate (fig. 3-57) and rose up a significant hill to the Rotunda at the top (fig. 3-58) and the sphere it enclosed, like understanding itself. The progress to the Rotunda was animated by a succession of instructive pavilions on either side of a rectangular terraced lawn joined by the contin-

uous run of a colonnade. Modeled on the Château de Marly (fig. 3-59)—with the mind, not the king, at the top of its hierarchy—Jefferson's plan had the crucial difference that the pavilions were carefully spaced so that the gaps between them grew greater as they descended with the lawn. Spreading out to the west, the pavilions reached out to the wilderness. Closing together in the other direction, they drew it back up into the control of the university and resolved it in the sphere of the Rotunda, much the way Jefferson himself sent out and brought back Lewis and Clark. Like a tool drawn for Diderot's Encyclopedia, Jefferson's mechanism was designed to serve a Republic embracing its future, bringing about its absorption and mastery by the enlightened mind.

Jefferson's device—the importance particularly of its orientation and open-endedness—was understood and respected when it was significantly expanded in the 1850s. Robert Mills attached a long addition to what was clearly the back of the Rotunda, leaving the lawn still open to the lane, the riders, and the farm animals to the west (fig. 3-60). But when Mills's addition burned in 1895 and took with it Jefferson's Rotunda, times had changed. The university's governing Board of Visitors now wanted an architecture that could serve a very different late-nineteenth-century America, an imperial America of white Beaux-Arts buildings and white fleets. Interestingly, McKim, Mead & White started with a scheme, now lost, that would have kept Jefferson's lawn open, to protect what they saw as the beautiful vista at the end of the campus. This the Visitors specifically rejected. The change they wanted, and got, was more fundamental. The scheme reversed the university's entire orientation, so that it faced not the western frontier but the east and Europe. Grand steps now led directly from the street up to the east portico of the Rotunda, like an authority to be consulted, not a state of enlightenment to be achieved by a process of

110

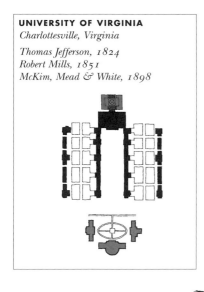

UNIVERSITY OF VIRGINIA
Charlottesville, Virginia

Thomas Jefferson, 1824
Robert Mills, 1851
McKim, Mead & White, 1898

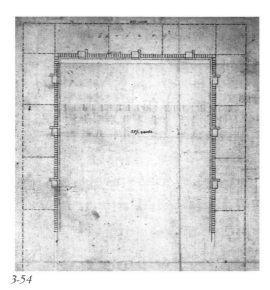

3-54

3-54. Thomas Jefferson's original conception of the University of Virginia

3-55. Jefferson's sketch energized by Benjamin Latrobe

3-56. The official plan of Jefferson's educational mechanism opening to the west

3-57. The rustic gate at the entry to the process of enlightenment

3-58. The heavens smile on the result

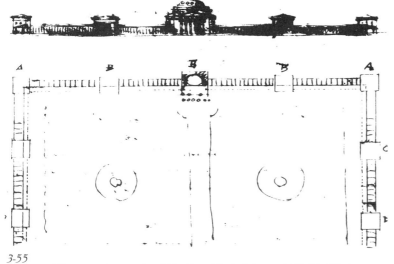

3-55

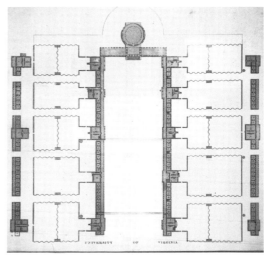

3-56

3-57

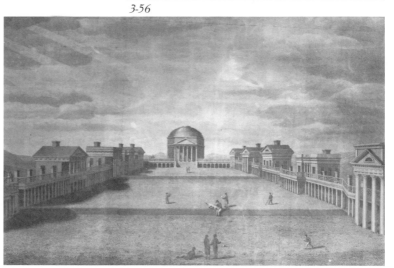

3-58

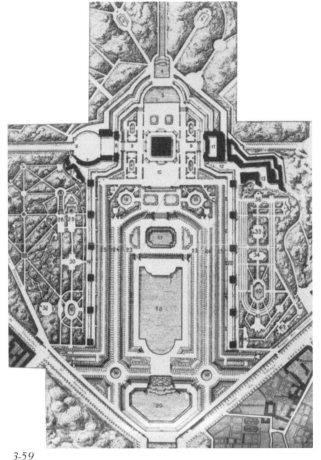

3-59

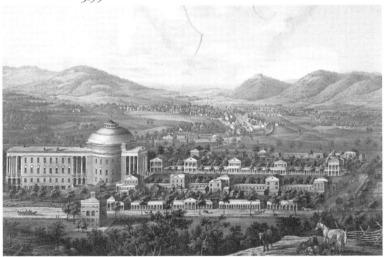

3-60

3-59. *The authoritarian antecedent: the Château de Marly*

3-60. *Robert Mills's addition (left) understands Jefferson's idea and backs it up*

education (fig. 3-61). Jefferson's device was now behind the Rotunda, a subordinate appendage, and, crucially, it was closed (fig. 3-62). Stanford White's new groups of buildings were wrapped around the open end of the Lawn at a little distance, with the new Cabell Hall right in the middle to shut it down. Jefferson's open and original American plan was now absorbed in a larger closed, symmetrical European Beaux-Arts diagram (fig. 3-63), a relatively pompous and conventional representation of a closed body of knowledge imposed by authority. The new diagram was interesting for the contrast of its authoritative system as well as the circumstances of its imposition. The Beaux-Arts plan was set up as a model for American planning by the Columbian Exposition of 1893, the great American celebration of coming of age and self-assertion as a world power. The nation no longer aimed at its west but at Europe and the world, ready to emulate and compete. Lecturing in Chicago at the time of the exposition, Frederick Jackson Turner announced the closing of the American frontier. When White's plan came down on the Lawn, the frontier closed for Jefferson as well.

White went to considerable pains to control the impact of his changes. He created Cabell Hall to address the Rotunda face to face, but as a subordinate element. He used the slope of the Lawn to lower Cabell's height and made it a single, flat rectangle with none of the focal power of the domed sphere of the Rotunda—indeed, a form squashed as if it were embarrassed and trying to keep its head down. All the new buildings were detailed with classical ornamentation more archeological and less inventive than Jefferson's. The damage, however, was done in the change of orientation and the compromise of the extraordinary idea Jefferson expressed in the expanding organization of the Lawn. That idea, while still discernible through the trees in the special spacing of the pavilions beside the Lawn,

3-61

3-61. The little statue of Jefferson makes the Rotunda seem even more mighty and authoritative

3-62. McKim, Mead & White's Beaux-Arts plan shuts down Jefferson

3-63. The University reversed and closed

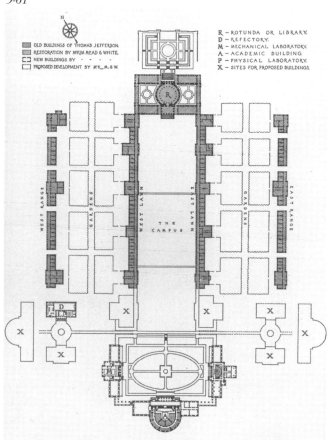

3-62

3-63

3-64. *Louis I. Kahn's Salk Institute on the edge of the Pacific.*

3-65. *Model of the facing bars of the plan with trees still in between*

3-66. *Between the bars, the Institute's horizon*

3-67. *For purposes of an addition, an early misunderstanding of Kahn's plan*

3-68. *The final misunderstanding*

3-69. *The elegant façades of the addition open a direct way to the central space*

was no longer the controlling idea, the idea at the top of the hierarchy of ideas, the one that forced the organization of all the rest. Traces remained, like fossils, but the idea itself was dead.

SALK INSTITUTE

Louis Kahn's extraordinary plan parti for the Salk Institute in La Jolla, California (fig. 3-64), is as fundamental to its design as the organization of the lawn is to the University of Virginia. Much of the design's power derives from the plan consisting simply of two rectangular blocks of laboratories addressing each other broadside across a flat-floored open space (fig. 3-65). The space is crucially open at both ends, framing the sky, the horizon, and the flat Pacific Ocean at one end and, through the veil of a eucalyptus grove, the mountains and the American continent at the other. Exposure to this open-endedness makes the space no less than awesome, a pause between two infinites. Viewed in plan, the two opposing complex blocks charge the space with significance like the target of a particle accelerator.

Experienced in three dimensions, the union of space and light is an exposition of meaning in a class with the Parthenon. A delicate imbalance within the double-ended open space brings its meaning out. The entry at the eastern end is higher than the west, making it more closed and the west more open. Access to the eastern entry includes a climb that is part of a process of introduction and progressive revelation. The grove of scraggly eucalyptus to the east serves as a collector as Bernini's colonnade does for Saint Peter's pilgrims, screening the access and filtering out the banality of the ordinary world left behind. Multiple footpaths through the filtering grove approach at angles, climbing and turning in an oblique disclosure first of the sacred space and then of the full view. From the

3-64

3-65

entry the space addresses the west. The repeated pavilions on either side turn to the west; the central Alhambra-like watercourse flows to a western cascade. Shown off in the west is the infinite horizon framed and engaged like the prospective work of the Institute (fig. 3-66).

Anshen + Allen's 1995 plans for the addition start with an apparent misunderstanding of the importance of Kahn's single-axis plan parti. Their successive design proposals all cross the eastern end of the open double I with a conflicting axis at right angles—rectangular buildings in line of battle fatally crossing the T. The successive designs then all take control of the crucial point of intersection at the head of the hierarchy in a new U plan. The most obvious of these designs puts an outdoor rotunda at the intersection like the domes or other focal monuments that commonly dominate similar plans (fig. 3-67). The rotunda marks and controls a new formal entry into the Salk by way of a new single-axial approach straight on to the great space. With the rotunda the combination becomes a different, much more conventional plan—almost a cliché—with the addition taking charge of the new combined plan hierarchy and reducing the original blocks to a pair of pendant wings.

In the face of criticism of the scheme, Anshen + Allen suppressed the rotunda and moved the new buildings farther back from the originals. Although handed an alternative plan that would have deferred to Kahn's, they nevertheless insisted on imposing their new axis. The intersection of the axes became a flat entry plaza between the end façades of two new buildings set at right angles to the original. In front of each of these, concrete segments of circles face each other (fig. 3-68), picking up on the face-to-face relationship of Kahn's bars beyond and offering a version of it like glow-plugs at the high point of the imposed new hierarchy (fig. 3-69).

3-66

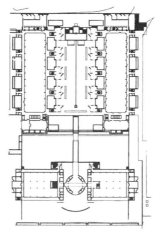

3-67

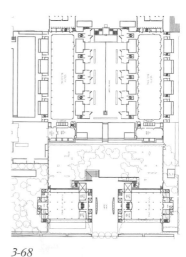

3-68

3-69

115

3-70

3-71

3-70. *The pieces of the addition seem to want to be garages*

3-71. *The cars and the parking lot made part of the composition*

3-72. *Kahn's suggestion for appropriate additions*

3-72

The expression of the addition compounds this imposition of ordinariness. At the official entry the wealthy elegance of the new façades presumes to stand for Kahn's simplicity, its very different elegance of wealth and technique set up against his elegance of fitness and economy of means. The long dimensions of the new low rectangles run along the edge of the enlarged parking lot with elevations striped horizontally, as if the new buildings wanted to be garages (fig. 3-70). Inside the new flat entry plaza, a wide white set of stone steps exposes the sequence to Kahn's central space from the very first instant to every car (fig. 3-71). Cutting away the protective filter of the grove, the addition imposes its banality on the awesome strangeness of the Salk, demoting the masterwork as Mussolini did Saint Peter's.

In all this the addition seems obdurately wrongheaded. Kahn proposed partis for buildings that pointed the way to something more appropriate, notably his proposed cluster of residences so obviously strung loosely off to the side, way down the compositional hierarchy from the formal central space (fig. 3-72). The institute's own shaggy annex buildings are likewise still there to show the virtues of informality and self-suppression in the face of the sublime.

Master Plans

The plans of the University of Virginia and the Salk Institute were essential to their identities as works of art, and both were upset by unsympathetic additions. A variant problem is presented by plans expected to grow over time, where the identity of the original work becomes the source of principles for future growth like a master plan. McKim, Mead & White's 1893 design for Columbia University was expected to be built out by other hands, though not necessarily to accommodate change at the orders

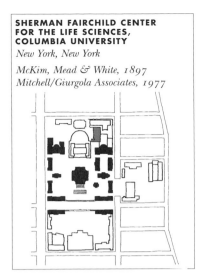

**SHERMAN FAIRCHILD CENTER
FOR THE LIFE SCIENCES,
COLUMBIA UNIVERSITY**
New York, New York

McKim, Mead & White, 1897
Mitchell/Giurgola Associates, 1977

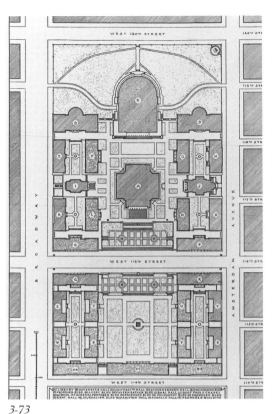

3-73

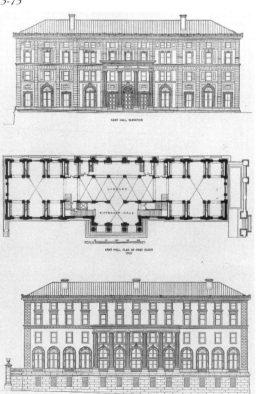

3-74

*3-73. McKim, Mead
& White's Plan for
Columbia University*

*3-74. The plan's
basic academic build-
ing block*

of magnitude required by the succeeding century. The same architects' vast 1897 Brooklyn Museum was designed to be built at one time but quickly became a master plan under the great weight of its ambition.

SHERMAN FAIRCHILD CENTER FOR THE LIFE SCIENCES, COLUMBIA UNIVERSITY

The commanding design for Columbia is worked out in detail as if the campus were a single building (fig. 3-73). It places the campus on a heroic platform at the top of Morningside Heights, some of the highest land in New York City. It fixes a relatively small rectangular block as the basic unit of academic building (fig. 3-74) and arranges a great number of them with closely comparable blocklike open spaces in a tight geometrical border around a field of larger open spaces and mid-size buildings for chapels and gyms, gridded by primary and secondary circulation paths. It lays out the whole in the clearest possible hierarchy of size and spacing up to the controlling cranium of Low Library, placed at the center in the round. The library is sited at the highest elevation at the top of a wide stair (fig. 3-75).

3-75

3-76

3-75. Low Library at the top of the plan's hierarchy

3-76. James Gamble Rogers's respectful Butler Library

The uniqueness of the campus plan is in its intended density and urbanness, the way it cuts up *rus* and *urbe* and repacks them as units in a device specifically to fit the university to the city. The repeated basic blocks are horizontal, with unbroken cornices brought to a single line, an upper datum tying the whole together under an open sky. The materials, the sizes of openings, and the sizes and abundance of detail on the blocks are prescribed so that they will be varied but similar, large enough to be read together across the largest open spaces, and assertive enough so that their lessons are not missed.

As long as spaces fitting in these blocks satisfied the university, the plan could be filled out by subsequent architects working within its conventions. Many of the blocks were actually by McKim, Mead & White. Other blocks were distinguishable only in the ways their architects handled the same conventions. Significantly, only one of the proposed perimeter sets of blocks and open spaces was built, where the plan's ultimate assumptions about density could be tested by experience. The addition of the South Campus doubled the area controlled by the plan, the large, central open space and the new buildings around it maintaining the primacy of Low above them. Directly opposite Low at the bottom of the extended campus, the low, wide rectangle and colonnade of James Gamble Rogers's Butler Library closed the South Campus with a strong but subordinate form (fig. 3-76). To either side, however, dormitories began to stretch the plan's assumptions about the height of the basic block, keeping their dimensions and detail close to the original design even while breaking the perceptual horizon and cutting into the sky.

After World War II, faced with programmatic needs for kinds and quantities of space never imagined by the plan, modernist architects of the 1950s and 1960s began to aggregate spaces into simpler, bigger, taller lumps with new shapes (fig. 3-77). These lumps overrode the scale of the original blocks, blotted out the pattern of the plan, and, in their abhorrence of ornament, stripped away the visual glue of its detail. The bloated boxes of Ferris Booth, Seeley Mudd, and Uris halls—Uris was nominated at the time New York's worst building of the year—at the beginning, middle, and end of the campus condescended to the plan as they blanked out large chunks of its intended experience.

Two major proposals tried to develop the plan in ways that would help it take into account the university's needs for different kinds and quantities of space. In the early 1960s Wallace Harrison tried to extend it to a new East Campus accommodating fatter building blocks on an inflated platform, building out in the process every then-current misunderstanding about the organization of cities and the social uses of streets and open space. I. M. Pei and Partners' plan for development of the South Campus was much more sensitive and interesting. Conceived in response to violent student protest in 1968 at the university's design for a gym in the adjacent public park, Pei's plan sought to respect the campus by building underground. Above ground he proposed a pair of towers at either side of the steps up to Low, new forms that might have been acceptable within the plan's hierarchy in the relative freedom of the South Campus (fig. 3-78). Like Pei's small tower at the Massachusetts Institute of Technology, these new blocks began to explore height as a source of expansion within the plan, with slenderness offering a way to make the basic block bigger without impairing the plan's intended openness to the sky.

When the crisis subsided, Pei's plan was quickly suppressed and his towers forgotten. Thereafter, in the 1970s and 1980s, the university undertook a number of building

3-77

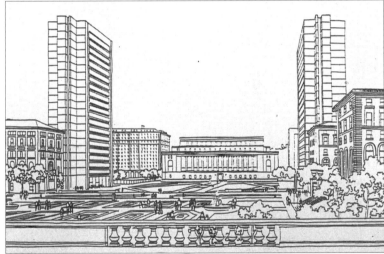

3-78

3-77. *Awkward, oblivious Ferris Booth Hall*

3-78. *I. M. Pei suggested a way height might be used to make room for expansion*

*3-79. Mitchell/
Giurgola devise a
way to slip a big
block into the
plan*

*3-80. A complex
response to the
plan helps resolve
the axis*

3-79

3-80

projects that seriously engaged the full range of its ideas. Mitchell/Giurgola Architects' Fairchild Center did best in resurrecting the intention of the plan. Fairchild is a rectangular block like the basic building block of the plan, but bigger in order to meet current standards for laboratory space and raised on a smaller footprint to fit beside a major open circulation axis of the plan (fig. 3-79). To control the resulting bulge over the axis, Giurgola screens the end and sides with panels of tile, extending the end panel over the campus axis and dropping a long stair down it on the far side. The screen and the stair bring out some of the complexity of the axis as a system of movement and as an element in the plan. Emphasizing the direction, linearity, and movement of the axis, the long parallel stair makes an event of the lift and turn by which one leaves the axis to get into the buildings. While the axis might originally have shot off the podium into the sky, Seeley Mudd Hall had made it end in indistinct vistas of brick. Giurgola's screen now gives the axis a complex new terminal event, even as the walk itself continues underneath to the space beyond (fig. 3-80)—a layering of spaces comparable to the layering of the original plan. Here and elsewhere on Fairchild, Giurgolas's screen panels give the façade an additional thickness to show off with a play of light and shadow openings that could read at the scale of the campus and tie it together in the manner expected by the plan. At the same time the screens calls attention, in their abstraction, to the artifice of the plan's instructive detailing.

The university's attitude to its principal work of art continued to evolve. The home of the nation's first graduate school of architectural preservation, Columbia imposed that discipline on itself only to a limited degree. Many little changes were allowed to weaken the intensity of the experience offered by surviving original buildings. Not long after Fairchild, the university lapsed back into a practice of building mediocrity. The lump of Shapiro Hall wears imitations of the details of the plan stuck on like gum. The plan itself continued to give satisfaction because of the great strength of the parts that were built, which continued to dominate the experience of Columbia's central and identifying place. At the same time it never got the chance to show the full effect of its intended approach to the problem of density, burdened as its central experience was by the banalities of the 1950s and 1960s.

BROOKLYN MUSEUM OF ART

While McKim, Mead & White's Columbia University campus had attributes of a master plan from the start, their Brooklyn Museum design became a master plan only when circumstances required that it be developed in numerous phases. Columbia had the good fortune to start by building the most important and controlling elements of its plan, Low Library and its surroundings, which allowed the plan to survive subsequent changes. The Brooklyn Museum never got to its most important part, standing as a result throughout its history as a relatively incomprehensible, incomplete work. Then, in a competition for its completion, the museum got a winning scheme that understood the original and promised to give it even greater freedom, interest, and power than had first been conceived.

The original design was for an immense museum (fig. 3-81), a claim of importance for America's second largest city as a cultural center that was, however, soon deflated by Brooklyn's consolidation with New York in 1898. A large central dome presided over a square of four skylit quadrangles (fig. 3-82) with subsidiary domes and entries, the climax of a grand progress up a huge stair from Eastern Parkway leading into and through the museum.

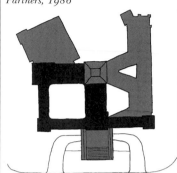

BROOKLYN MUSEUM OF ART
Brooklyn, New York

McKim, Mead & White, 1897
William Lescaze, 1935
Arata Isozaki/James Stewart Polshek & Partners, 1986

3-81. McKim, Mead & White's design for the Brooklyn Institute of Arts and Sciences

3-82. The mighty plan

3-81

3-82

3-83. The first piece built

3-84. As much as was built

3-85. With the removal of the stair, William Lescaze cut the museum back to scale with its reality, with the original like a great fragment on its back

3-83

3-84

3-85

Construction began with a relatively small fragment of the design (fig. 3-83). The fragment grew in a subsequent construction until it included the grand stair and almost all of the Eastern Parkway façade, a thick false front for a missing monument (fig. 3-84). The façade, with its grand stair and peculiar low dome, became both more and less mysterious when William Lescaze's 1940s renovation removed the grand stair, taking away an important clue to the larger design while ending the anomaly of a grand stair that didn't go anywhere worthy of its size (fig. 3-85). Patched in place of the stair's lower entry, Lescaze's plain modernist façade confirmed the reduced ambitions of the fragment.

In the heady 1980s the museum's ambitions revived, and it sponsored a competition for the completion of the building. The competition brief called attention to the importance of the old building and the original plan; it provided drawings of the plan and asked specifically for the restoration of the grand stair. While all the schemes substantially built up the old fragment, only the winning entry of Arata Isozaki/James Stewart Polshek & Partners made sense of it (fig. 3-86). At the critical central intersection of the original plan they placed a dramatic new building element—a truncated, light-gathering pyramid (fig. 3-87) like the original organizing dome but with the novelty of the work of Isozaki—thus honoring the original plan as the organizer of the old and the new and restoring the hierarchy originally proposed for the architecture of the whole institution. With an element of sufficient power in this place—a reminder, among other things, of the great dome that explained the fragment's little low one—the surviving fragment could get back into its place as the subordinate element it was originally intended to be and the grand stair could be reconstructed with a worthy destination (fig. 3-88) At the same time, added pieces that were dis-

122

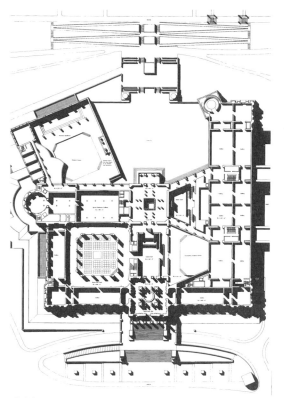

3-86

3-87

3-86. *Arata Isozaki and Associates/James Stewart Polshek and Partners' plan to redeem the original*

3-87. *Isozaki's truncated pyramid reoccupies the center of the plan*

3-88. *The grand stair comes back with somewhere to go*

3-88

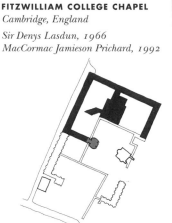

3-89. Sir Denys Lasdun's grim tempo-rary entry for Fitzwilliam College, Cambridge University

3-90. Lasdun's mushroom roof for the Hall inside

3-89

3-90

tinctly new could fall into place in new arrangements as required by their programs, by their necessary connections, and by the ambitions of their designers, all still under the eye of the original plan. The scheme thus resurrected and honored the original plan by building out its central idea and using its great strength to tie together the buildings and goals of the renewed museum.

Building Types

Additions are often made as increments within standard building types like colleges and cathedrals. The colleges of Cambridge University are accretions of particular pieces of program, repeated, varied combinations of bed/sitting rooms, masters' lodges, libraries, halls, chapels, and connecting galleries, greens and open spaces, all scaled to an ancient, intimate notion of scholarship and individual instruction central to the idea of the university. Over the years the colleges have grown in increments with pieces designed sometimes by anonymous ancient masons and sometimes by great architects like Wren and Hawksmoor. Among numerous pieces added recently, Richard MacCormac's chapel for Fitzwilliam College is interesting for the way it redeems a serious-minded, unprepossessing work of the 1960s. Another, Edward Cullinan's Saint John's Library, enriches one of the plainer portions of its historic host complex, but with a display that seems to undermine it.

FITZWILLIAM COLLEGE CHAPEL

British brutalism was a set of expressive choices for architecture in the 1960s that is hard to understand without reference to the now-fading nightmare of the atom bomb. The hard, repellent forms and desolate spaces of the brutalists seem gratuitous without the prospect of a nuclear Armageddon to make sense of them, as if their prefiguration of the worst were a way to stand up to it or even cure it.

Sir Denys Lasdun's application of these ideas to new buildings for Fitzwilliam in 1966 produced a version of the traditional college that seems literally, and possibly deliberately, appalling. Few entry elevations could be more repellent than the street façade that served as Fitzwilliam's temporary entry after the first section of the new college was built (fig. 3-89). The wall is stacks of black brick cut with continuous vertical window slots and one barely perceptible slot for entry, its unrelieved, uncontained length overridden by two endless fat, whitish stripes on the edges of its slabs. The wall greets the visitor with a prospect depressing enough to make even good bicycles look bent. Things improve a bit inside. The window slots are broken and offset at the slab edges, less roughly cut though more agitated between the stripes of the slab edges and against the sky. The walls enclose a landscaped court surrounding the college's principal architectural event, the college dining hall, the roof of which mushrooms up from central columns over glass clerestories, a little like the ghastly explosion it seems to anticipate (fig. 3-90).

Like other colleges, the ground plan of Fitzwilliam was laid out to accommodate expansion and to leave space for other buildings, like the neighboring Victorian villa that once belonged to the Darwin family and served Fitzwilliam as its master's lodge. Invited to add a chapel to Fitzwilliam in 1992, Richard MacCormac chose to attach the new building at the open end of Lasdun's central interior range of rooms, at the end of the run of rooms with a single smooth vertical brick bar that interrupts Lasdun's slab edge bands. Then, after a recess containing a square opening for the chapel entry, the stripes start up again as a relatively delicate pair on a surface that is now a smooth wall, not a stack of bricks. It

3-91

3-92

3-91. *Richard MacCormac's chapel attached to Lasdun's range in 1992*

3-92. *The enclosing form of the chapel*

3-93

3-93. The chapel window

3-94. The chapel's view of the tree and the Master's house

3-94

curves out uninterrupted, a segment of cylinder capped and closed with a white coping (fig. 3-91). The wall is Lasdun's surface and the stripe his stripe, but resolved at the end of his ragged run in a serene, proportioned, enclosing form (fig. 3-92).

The chapel is inside the cylinder, like something precious contained by hands in prayer. A delicate assembly of skylit blond shipbuilder's woodwork, the room addresses a glass wall behind the altar and through the glass a magnificent tree. The space contained is not easy to comprehend from outside because of its enclosure by the curved walls and because its glass face is almost buried in the long branches of the tree (fig. 3-93). This limited exposure emphasizes the privacy and intimacy of the experience inside and its contrast with the appalling spectacle contemplated by the original surrounding architecture. Inside, with elegant finishes drawn from nordic boats, MacCormac provides a refuge like an ark. With the calm form of the chapel holding the ark, he resolves Lasdun's ragged horror into a celebration of the life the chapel protects at the culmination of Lasdun's form (fig. 3-94).

MacCormac's chapel does something exceedingly difficult: it makes us take seriously an architecture we might otherwise readily write off. It explains both what Lasdun's original must have had in mind and what makes it worth taking seriously. For a building as unlikeable as Lasdun's, it is hard to imagine an addition doing more!

SAINT JOHN'S COLLEGE LIBRARY

At Saint John's College, Edward Cullinan enjoyed a huge head start over MacCormac at Fitzwilliam. The context of Cullinan's new library was unpretentious, the end of an existing range of good 1930s buildings running between a garden and the forecourt to the college's big Victorian chapel (fig. 3-95). Attached to the end of the range, his cruciform plan begins promisingly, its intersecting crossbar making the library the major event it deserves to be in the chapel court, the detached cylinder of a new stair providing a respectful end to the range (fig. 3-96).

The difficulties begin with the flat peaked end gable of the crossbar opposite the chapel. Intended as a suitably formal response to the end gable of the chapel and a reasonable assertion of the library's own importance, the gable end is highly ornamented against the plain background of the court (fig. 3-97). The surface of the court is sunk in front of the new façade to dignify the entry at the bottom and to focus on its expression. But, with all this emphasis, what one is supposed to pay attention to and understand from the expression is unclear. The strong base of the gable end dissolves on either corner into a curious wraparound assembly of white colonettes that end indistinctly at the top of the corners against the sky. In the middle is the formal gable end, topped by a peak that is a grander cousin of the old gable peak next to the library. The new end gable has an added Palladian hole to give it greater importance but is shown off as a sort of false front, without its neighbors' three-dimensional solidity. The end gable is centered on a tall, flat panel of brick like the panels that might elsewhere be poster boards for plaques or other commemorative ornaments, but a little too big and tall to work that way. The gable offers a great deal of attention-getting ornament, that is, but does not make clear its purpose or even whether it intends to be serious or amusing. The very prominent new library lantern with its ultralight metal base, cylindrical clerestory, funny-hat cone of disks, and hardware-store ceiling fan is neither funny enough to laugh at nor serious enough to appreciate. Disappointing in itself, it is worse for its neighbors: is it meant to suggest those other lanterns are just gewgaws too?

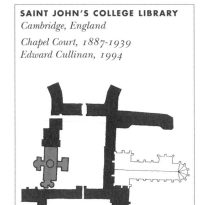

SAINT JOHN'S COLLEGE LIBRARY
Cambridge, England

Chapel Court, 1887-1939
Edward Cullinan, 1994

3-95. St. John's College Chapel Court

3-96. St. John's new library

3-95

3-96

3-97

The fact that the library's expression doesn't come to much would be simply disappointing if it were not for its self-important tendency to compete with, distract from, and even put down its neighbors. In a context like Cambridge—and perhaps anywhere—when one hasn't much to say, one should always remember the advantages of keeping still.

CATHEDRAL CHURCH OF SAINT JOHN THE DIVINE

The Cathedral Church of Saint John the Divine in New York shares the common characteristic of cathedrals—that they generally take a long time to complete and, accordingly, often reflect significant changes in architecture across their periods of construction (fig. 3-98). Saint John's has been relatively short abuilding—only a hundred years. On the other hand, its century has been particularly full of change, includ-

ing genuine uncertainty as to what cathedrals should mean and a dramatic increase in architectural possibilities for the expression of what that might turn out to be.

The competition for Saint John's offered a wide selection of styles, many of them wonderfully bizarre and all of them very big. The winner in 1891 was Hinz and LaFarge's Romanesque scheme, which seemed the most resolved and satisfactory architecturally (fig. 3-99). Actual building started slowly. The choir was built and then, amid differences and difficulties, LaFarge was squeezed out and the project taken over by the strong-willed Gothicist Ralph Adams Cram, who substituted a Gothic design (fig. 3-100). Parts of the Romanesque choir were gothicized at what must have been great expense, and a vast Gothic nave was added. Then Cram died, World War II began, and work stopped, with towers and transepts unbuilt, the crossing rough arched and closed with a wonderful temporary Guastavino vault, and the last vestige of an 1840 Greek Revival orphan asylum still nestled up against the wall where the south transept would go. In this form the cathedral became a protected landmark.

Schemes were offered from time to time for the cathedral's completion by its succeeding architects, Adams and Woodbridge, by students, and by others. In the late 1970s construction resumed from the cathedral's own stoneyard, following Cram's plan stone by stone, as a mixture of religious and community service. Then, in the late 1980s, when it seemed reasonable to rethink the overall plan in case building in earnest once again became possible, the completion of the cathedral became the subject of another design competition. This competition was particularly compelling, the church being interested in opening up its program. The competition brief sought to complete the cathedral with designs for a biosphere at its crossing to express reverence for biological life, stirring up architectural responses that

**CATHEDRAL CHURCH OF
SAINT JOHN THE DIVINE**
New York, New York

Heinz and LaFarge, 1891
Ralph Adams Cram, 1927
Santiago Calatrava, 1991

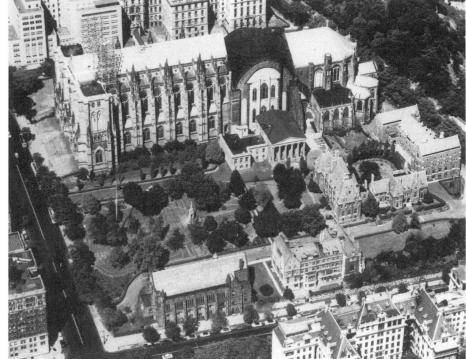

3-98

3-99

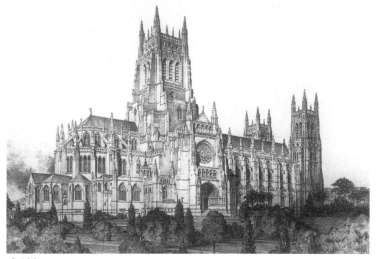

3-100

3-98. Saint John the Divine before the
latest building campaign

3-99. Heinz and LaFarge's original
winning design

3-100. Ralph Adams Cram
converted it to Gothic

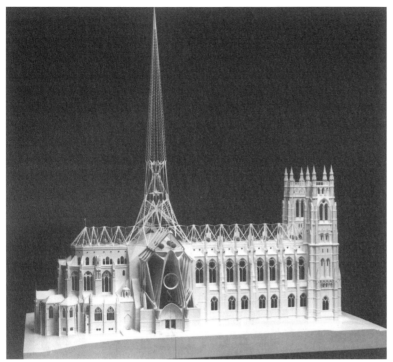

3-101

3-101. Model of Santiago Calatrava's skeletal scheme for completion

3-102. The bones of Calatrava's proposal

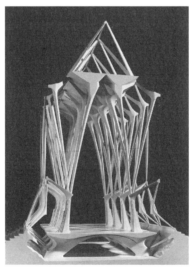

3-102

might not have been brought forth in a more conventional celebration of Episcopalianism, particularly with Cram's unimpeachable Gothic design already on the table.

The winning design of Santiago Calatrava took full advantage of the invitation, proposing an audacious, logical, bony structure in prestressed stone that would complete the crossing and fill the attic with trees. Above it all would rise a slender spire taller and more dramatic than those conceived by LaFarge and Cram (fig. 3-101). The proposal clearly evolved from the Gothic, with its stone at least theoretically all in compression, its slender legs resting in pairs along aisles, its voids pointed, and its overall thrust uncompromisingly skyward. At the same time, its very obvious bleached boniness seemed to reach beyond the Gothic toward an intricacy of design achieved only in skeletons by the relentless workings of evolution (fig. 3-106). It brought together the church and the biosphere in the thing it celebrated and in the built process of celebration, giving Darwin a powerful presence in the house of God.

Calatrava's addition would have brought to a climax the relatively rapid evolution of Saint John's, from the ancient darkness of LaFarge's Romanesque through the ambitious, if conventional, strength and lightness of Cram's Gothic to a structure possible only with the technology of the late twentieth century and carrying meanings beyond those of traditional religion. It brought along the old parts as honorable contributors in the hierarchy of a remarkable expression of its times, keeping them intact as appreciable parts but fulfilling their destiny as parts at last of a whole.

Calatrava's scheme threatened the "temporary" Guastavino dome and the Greek Revival orphan home. If the scheme had gone forward, the orphan home could have easily been moved to a position honoring it with new prominence—possibly replacing a goofy statue in the cathedral close at the head of an adjacent street. As for the dome, the notion that it was to be temporary could simply be accepted. Happily, the cathedral's incompleteness was not part of the identity protected by its designation. In the event, the conflict disappeared when the good times of the 1980s ceased to roll, the stoneyard closed, and Calatrava's scheme went on the shelf.

Adding On

Wings and dependent buildings are the commonest architectural additions. They affect the buildings to which they are attached by their expressive commentary.

THE OCTAGON

Mitchell/Giurgola Architects' ill-fated proposal for a building in the backyard of the Octagon, the elegant old headquarters of the American Institute of Architects in Washington, D.C., was the winner of a competition sponsored by the institute to give it needed space and, ideally, to transform its headquarters into a proper late-twentieth-century representation of the profession in the capital and in the nation. The building the institute ultimately built did both things, though the image of the profession it offered was not uplifting.

The starting point of the scheme was an elegant 1801 Federal townhouse by Dr. William Thornton, first architect of the Capitol, that derived its form from the truncated triangle of its site, a sharp corner on a wide avenue across from a park near the White House (fig. 3-103). A semicylindrical central tower containing its octagonal entry hall marked the apex of the triangle and joined two short, rectangular wings, the whole set off from its neighbors by a large garden. The prominent, long public surface of any addition at the bottom and beyond

THE OCTAGON
Washington D.C.

Dr. William Thornton, 1801
Mitchell/Giurgola & Associates,
1965–1978

3-103

3-103. Dr. William Thornton's Octagon House

3-104

3-105

3-104. Mitchell/
Giurgola's visionary
proposal for an addi-
tion

3-105. The glass
wall focused
on the Octagon

3-106. A sketch of
the experience inside

3-106

the garden would speak for the institute with the force of a billboard.

Giurgola's winning design left the old house and the garden untouched, the three-story addition filling the back of the site against its two side street walls and its bent rear property line (fig. 3-104). The enclosure of the addition was brick, an opaque, abstract three-dimensional form starting with small elements on the street wall at the edge of the gap made by the garden and building up to a high wall along the property line. This solid enclosure held the extraordinary feature that completed the scheme and tightly bound the old and new together—a tall, delicate segment of a large sphere in glass curving all the way across the front of the addition and focusing in all three dimensions on the old house in front of it (fig. 3-105). The wall was most obviously and, to begin with, a setting—almost a socket—for the house. As a unifying geometry for the combination, the sphere honored and expanded upon the circle that unified the plan of the old house and gave it its name and its identity. As glass, it made immediate expressive connections with the old building by its multiple panes and by its inescapable associations with elegance and fragility. By its transparency, the glass brought the old house into the new building, kept it always in sight, its recurrent image continuing to control the open space and the new interior (fig. 3-106). As a piece of technical audacity, the glass wall evoked the new orders of possibility opening to architects in the twentieth century. At the same time, like an astronomer's mirror, the wall resolved its explorations in the old house that it celebrated as its objective and protected with the embrace of its curve.

The design offered the institute a wonderful combined work as its representative display. The addition engaged and showed off against its freedom and abstraction the simplicity, elegance, and fragility of an exemplary old artifact. It made the old building the formal focus of a statement about the responsibilities and possibilities of architecture in its time, about what it should strive for and what it should cherish. In its combination of adventure, respect, and truth it could have been a proposition of the highest order about architecture.

The proposal ran into professional politics and a failure of the professional imagination. Under pressure from those who didn't understand the scheme and possibly also shared its architect's uncertainties about how to build the glass wall, Giurgola made four subsequent proposals intended to save what he could of its meaning while reducing its audacity (fig. 3-107). The increasingly solid alternatives with increasingly orthogonal geometries all tended to weigh against and cut off the old building and reduce its control of and contribution to the combined meaning (fig. 3-108). Each fell further away from the organizing innovation of the original scheme.

After the fourth revision, Giurgola resigned. A successor pressed on notwithstanding in the direction preferred by the institute and produced a result of outstanding ordinariness, a building just like a developer's speculative office development anywhere in Washington, D.C. The old building gave up precious ground to the crude commercial assumptions of its context and wound up fending for itself in front of an aggressive, heavy concrete and glass wall of strip windows (fig. 3-109). The developer beyond the garden was sniffing at the back of the house.

The result prefigured changing times—waning confidence in the new and a sometimes disproportionate respect for the old. As a billboard for the institute the addition turned out to be dismally apt: the professional association made a bow to historic building conservation—the easy part of preservation—and publicly confirmed its basic allegiance to money and business.

3-107

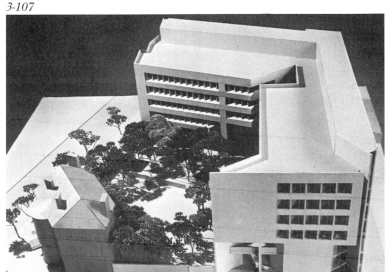

3-108

3-109

3-107. A simpler wall and a harsher frame

3-108. The glass almost gone

3-109. The American Institute of Architects cradled in real estate development

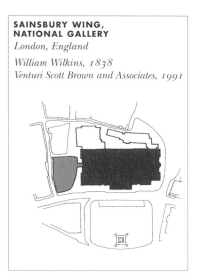

3-110. Venturi and Scott Brown's
Sainsbury Wing of the National
Gallery, London

3-111. William Wilkins's National
Gallery

3-110

3-111

134

SAINSBURY WING, NATIONAL GALLERY

The Sainsbury Wing, Venturi Rauch and Scott Brown's 1991 addition to Britain's National Gallery on Trafalgar Square in London (fig. 3-110), affects both an important building—the 1838 landmark by William Wilkins—and an important place, Trafalgar Square, the heroic public space Wilkins's building defines and, in its slightly eccentric presence, helps ennoble.

Wilkins's long building stretches across the entire upper side of Trafalgar Square, with the baroque royal chapel of Saint Martin's-in-the-Fields at one corner and the site of the Sainsbury Wing at the other (fig. 3-111). Replacing the earlier King's Gallery, Wilkins's classical building created a procession of new galleries and gave the royal collection enhanced presence in the growing city. Divided and ordered by applied domed porticoes that build up to a central entry under a skinny central dome, the building never enjoyed great critical success. Wilkins himself defended what he acknowledged was its plainness as a consequence of a need to address Saint Martin's-in-the-Field with proper humility.

Venturi Rauch and Scott Brown's winning competition entry attaches the new wing at the end of Wilkins's long façade after a slot at the corner for a small pedestrian street. Its principal façade extends the apparent plane of Wilkins's façade as an irregularly bent surface down Pall Mall and out of the square. The façade is a sheet of white Portland stone cut with entries and windows and decorated with bands, pilasters, capitals, and window-surrounds closely related to Wilkins's (fig. 3-112). Its composition is densest near Wilkins and dwindles away down the street. The Pall Mall façade is the building's most developed. Starting at the next corner, succeeding façades of the wing offer distinctly dif-

3-112

3-113

ferent expressions responding to the buildings they face, their own functions, and and their relative importance in the overall scheme of the wing (fig. 3-113).

Like the addition to the Allen Memorial Art Museum at Oberlin (see chapter 2), the Sainsbury Wing is, in Venturi's terms, a decorated shed. It depends for its effect not so much on the observer's immediate, visceral response to its three-dimensional form—indeed one critic thought it formless enough to call it a scumbag—but on its success in inducing the observer to read what it

3-112. The plain entries and the fancy pilasters of the addition

3-113. The façade become plainer as it turns the corner

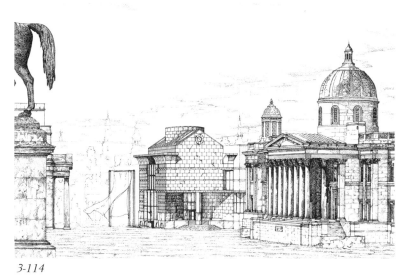

3-114

3-114. James Stir-
ling's alternate
proposal

is saying and absorb its argument. The argument composed on Trafalgar Square is
made of bits that are variously plain (the
square cut entries, for example) and fancy
(perfect classical pilasters and capitals). It
uses abstraction to show off its bits—and, by
reference, Wilkins's bits as well—as artifices
properly represented and freely used as
such in a twentieth-century addition. The
palette of the façade is subdued, like that of
the original building, and has a certain high
seriousness to fit a national gallery rather
than a college art museum. Its formlessness
seems to make a point of Wilkins's deference, dissolving his decoration and attentu-
ating his form so that the extended whole
peters out down Pall Mall, becoming less
clearly defined and less clearly defining the
corner of Trafalgar Square.

The choice of this design over other
competition entries clearly attached high
value to the interest of the expression as
commentary on Wilkins and as a manifestation of the important ideas contributed
by Venturi Rausch and Scott-Brown to
twentieth-century architectural theory.
This confidence in the value of the commentary may have been reinforced by the

historic ambiguity about Wilkins's building, as if its eccentricity argued for an
expression that might address it in a complex and cerebral way.

The questions the design raises have to
do in part with its high seriousness—for
example, the lack of the humor evident in
other works of the architects that might
have relieved the harshness of its abstracted entry openings—possibly the wing's
most hated feature—and made its argument more engaging. Like an American on
best behavior abroad, it lacks spontaneity.
More important is the impact of its relative
formlessness on its context, of its choice to
rely heavily on an appeal to the mind in a
very public place. In such a place, not the
learned corner of a college, omitting a
form that could be seized intuitively by the
ordinary eye—the refusal to supply a new
player for the muscle-flexing of other
buildings on Trafalgar Square—seems a
misjudgment of the work to be protected.
The Sainsbury's light, reflective stone and
animated surface are indeed compelling to
the eye, arguably intended to do with
words what others might have done with
form. But a significant difference remains
between reading a message and perceiving
a form, between a billboard and a building.
The Sainsbury corner of Trafalgar Square
needs something, again in Venturi's terms,
a little more "ducklike," for example, like
James Stirling's losing competitive design
(fig. 3-114). Wilkins's form seems weakened by the Sainsbury's emphasis on argument when it might have been strength-
ened by the end bracket of Stirling's eccentric corner pavilion. The square seems
weakened where its northern wall peters
out and its space leaks away, when a
stronger form might have more clearly
defined it, the way Saint Martin's does. At
the moment, as Sainsbury's once-arresting
"words" become familiar, its appeal even to
the mind seems on the wane.

WHIG AND CLIO

Additions are also commonly insertions directly into the body of a work of art, entering into the play of a three-dimensional composition and changing its meaning.

Immediately behind Princeton University's Nassau Hall are two campus landmarks, an unusual matched pair of virtually windowless Ionic temples, Whig and Clio halls (fig. 3-115). Designed in 1893 by A. Page Brown, they copy in marble two wooden temples from the 1830s that represented the two clubs into which the student body was divided in 1765. The clubs provided for students like James Madison and Aaron Burr a focus for the raucous competitive interaction of ideas central to their pursuit of wisdom under Princeton's early curriculum. The Delphic temple was an obvious choice for the form of their treasuries and shrines, safes for the sometimes jejeune secrets that defined them as societies. Their location right behind Nassau Hall reflected their importance—and the importance of argument—in the university's intellectual structure. Apart and precisely equal in marble, Brown's temples cleaned up and ennobled for late-nineteenth-century sensibilities the original coffeehouse brawl that underpinned education and government in the early republic.

The marble buildings actually represent a petrification of the societies near their apogee. Their influence was already declining in the 1890s and they were a generation out of their old business when Whig burned in 1969. Gwathmey Siegel started restoration of a shell lacking its east wall. They left unchanged its three surviving sides—the columned temple front addressing Nassau Hall, the west façade facing Clio, and the plain south façade, which was part of the composition the two temples made with Nassau Hall—but took advantage of the

WHIG AND CLIO
Princeton, New Jersey

A. Page Brown, *1893*
Gwathmey Siegel Associates, 1974

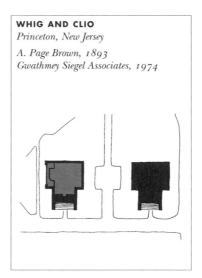

3-115

3-115. A. Page Brown's Whig and Clio Halls, surviving representatives of Princeton University's original combative curriculum

3-116

3-117

3-116. Whig Hall after the fire, with its addition

3-117. The addition's display of what's going on

destruction of the east wall to make major changes that would be seen from an important circulation axis of the campus (fig. 3-116). They retained the base and cornice of the east wall but removed its central field of stone, converting the ends of the sidewalls into square columns and the façade into a frame open to the sky, an outdoor proscenium with a pipe-rail just a little in from the edge (fig. 3-117). On the new stage they displayed the flat side wall of a new auditorium built inside the building. The surface of the modernist insertion was flat, white, and unadorned, much like the original stone wall but set off as an event by reveals on either side. The straight one stabilized the composition at the back south wall. The curved one animated the display, turning in behind the temple front with a suggestion of entry and exposure, revealing in a trophy case inside, the essence of debate as something to be won or lost.

The changes exposed meanings of the old institution in new ways. The new proscenium frame and the handsome architectural display within it called attention to the theatrical side of the old debates. The exclusivity of the hall was maintained by the wall and the height of the stage; there was no new entry or easy way in. As for its internal mysteries, the new blank white wall gave away few of them, though it did, by the very fact of the intervention, suggest that something important was once again going on inside, something that mattered to the university. The new design left alone the contribution the pair of buildings otherwise made to the campus. The buildings and the compositions they made could still be seen, just as they had always been, from every angle but one. From that angle, however, the temples and the societies were attached to the campus in a new way and once again alive.

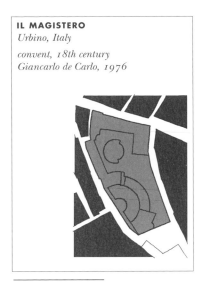

IL MAGISTERO

In his design for Il Magistero, the school of education in the ancient city of Urbino, Giancarlo De Carlo uses its site as if he were simply sticking his fingers in the city's poché. With his thumb he presses out the big curve of a lecture hall skylight; then, with his forefinger, he pokes down a smaller circular skylight for an open air court. The design seems perfectly to understand the city's density and the orientation of the buildings that give it its particular relationship to its context (fig. 3-118). The block occupied by the school is near the heart of the walled hill city, halfway up the slope to the basilica at the top (fig. 3-119). The block was vacant but perfectly enclosed by the walls of the convent that had occupied it. De Carlo filled the void with building, shaping his theater lecture hall and circular open space as new voids within it. In profile the building followed the topography of the city, with grassy roof terraces stepping downhill, all roughly within the descending plane set by the heights of the walls at the top and bottom, with no new intrusion into the sky. Cut into the slope of the roof, the principal curve of the theater skylight (fig. 3-120) looks out over the surrounding countryside, with its back to the protective hill, just as other buildings in the city have for centuries.

3-118

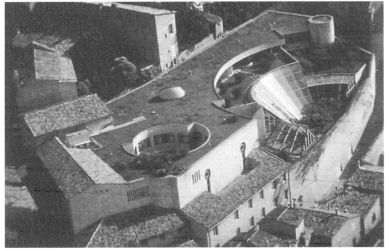

3-119

3-120

3-118. *Giancarlo di Carlo's Il Magistero on the hillside in Urbino*

3-119. *The punched-out poché*

3-120. *Il Magistero looks out from the hill*

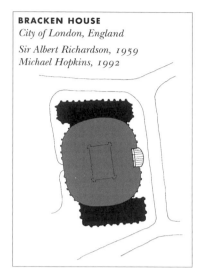

BRACKEN HOUSE
City of London, England

Sir Albert Richardson, 1959
Michael Hopkins, 1992

3-121

3-122

3-121. Sir Michael Hopkins's upgrade of Sir Albert Richardson's printing plant

3-122. The original printing plant

BRACKEN HOUSE

Michael Hopkins's evisceration of Sir Albert Richardson's Financial Times headquarters in London is a rare quantifiable success as an improvement of a historic building by radical change (fig. 3-121). After Hopkins carved out and replaced the entire center of the old building, its official classification as a historic monument actually rose by one whole grade!

The original building, built in the 1950s, consisted of two not-quite-parallel bars of office sandwiching the newspaper's central printing plant (fig. 3-122), an awkward amalgam of an industrial center and formal end façades, one of which faced Saint Paul's Cathedral and had the building's understated front door. Modeled on the Palazzo Carignano in Turin (fig. 3-123), Bracken House was nevertheless listed as a monument. Its appealing, corniceless classicism and nicely proportioned and detailed windows and brickwork reasonably represented the still powerful newspaper after the war.

When the paper sold the building for development in the 1980s, Hopkins removed the printing plant altogether and, with the Palazzo Carignano still in mind, substituted a new, taller central ellipse of office space that changed the orientation of the building away from Saint Paul's, giving it new strength as a form, a new public face, and a more convincing front door on its wide side. The powerfully expressed structure of the added ellipse elevates the industrial printing plant to something equally strong but much more elegant (fig. 3-124). Divided in a rhythm like that of the office wings, vertical steel substructures and connections exposed on the façade collect loads as they descend, growing in size and finally bearing on short, strong columns at the ground level. In the center of the façade the descent of the verticals is interrupted and transferred in a display of structural muscle and agility to make an opening for a dramatic glass canopy over the new front door. Between the structural assemblies the floors are glazed in three-part, full-height bay windows like Richardson's but also like the windows of early Chicago office buildings. The structure and window frames are dark brown next to Richardson's dark red-brown brick.

Hopkins's steel structure is oversized to avoid the need for added fireproofing and to satisfy his aesthetic requirement that elements bearing heavy loads show what they are doing. Its apparent strength equally brings out in a refined form appropriate to a modern office the strength inherent in Richardson's original idea of the working palazzo, a proper descendant of the fortresses of renaissance financiers. The surviving original wings are still subordinate parts, as they were in the original, but subordinate now to a more successful expression of the original idea. The fact that the scheme maintains the expression of the end façades undoubtedly contributed to the building's good reception, a kind of sigh of relief that at least one reasonably good neighbor of Saint Paul's would not be replaced by something worse. More important was the improvement over Richardson's building. That his work should be thus elevated by Hopkins would surely have pleased a generous and public-spirited if combative old gentleman.

3-123

3-124

3-123. Turin's Palazzo Carignano: model for the plant

3-124. The new canopy and entrance

141

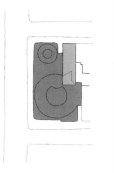

3-125. Frank Lloyd Wright's Guggenheim Museum: the free plan coiled up for a tight site

3-126. The Guggenheim standing up to the boxes

GUGGENHEIM MUSEUM

Frank Lloyd Wright's ornery 1960 Guggenheim Museum is a grand assertion of a particularly American kind of freedom. On the tight site on Fifth Avenue, Wright unleashed his favorite free plan, wrapping it around and into the great tipped spiral of the rotunda to generate a mighty way out of the city grid, beating the box and thumbing his nose at conventional, square New York (figs. 3-125 and 3-126). As with other free plans at the Robie House (fig. 3-127) and Fallingwater (fig. 3-128), he anchored the composition in place to make it work—but only just (fig. 3-129). The power of the Guggenheim's free form bankrupted its builder and tortures its curators to this day.

The museum's uneasy accommodation with its titanic work of art over the years resulted in various compromises, notably the filling in of Wright's little rotunda, a kind of starter-motor for the great one, with offices. When an ambitious museum administration decided in the 1980s to take on more broadly what it conceived as deficiencies of the building, it offered to restore the little rotunda as public space. It also decided to take on the big one.

Gwathmey Siegel's addition rose from the slot at the northeast border of the site occupied by a small, earlier addition designed by Wesley Peters, a Wright disciple. Against this boundary Wright himself had sketched a possible dormitory addition, probably more to improve the backdrop for his mighty museum than as a serious proposal for expansion. Generating anything like a useful piece of gallery and office space in this location required that the addition become substantially thicker than Wright's sketch, with the addition thus beginning to overhang the original. It also required that it connect directly into the rotunda.

The first proposal for the addition was in two parts, a flat background plane with a box of space hung in front and partially over the Museum (fig. 3-130). The breakdown in

3-125

3-126

3-127

3-127. The Robie House: the free plan anchored by its chimney

3-128. The plan likewise anchored at Fallingwater

3-129. The Guggenheim anchored by the stair enclosure

3-128

3-129

3-130

3-130. *Gwathmey Siegel's first design for the addition reintroduces the box*

3-131. *The geometry of the box takes over*

3-132. *The box firmly in charge in the addition as built*

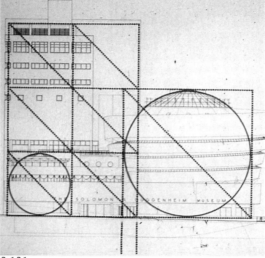

3-131

3-132

parts held the suspended box out as a new player in the composition, at the same time creating a shadow or reveal to mask the new joint with the rotunda. The scheme had the weakness that the new player was a box, not an obvious first choice to complement Wright no matter how many analytic diagrams might be constructed to try to lock them together (fig. 3-131). The scheme's fatal weakness, however, was that it resembled an old fashioned pull-chain water closet. The final design simplified the addition into a single, uniform, lightly gridded rectangular slab, still a box but intended as a sympathetic background and supplement to the forms of the original.

The new box, in fact, seems less like part of the work of art than an interfering, smooth curator with his hands all over it, showing it off to his friends (fig. 3-132). It crowds the site and reduces the freedom of the animated forms of the original. Worse, it shows off on its face the attachment of the rotunda, making the fact of its attachment a significant feature of the composition. Before the addition, the movement of the plan and the lift of the tipped spiral of the rotunda had been reconciled by the special, inflected mass that Wright specially designed to hold the combination. The mass ended in the sharp wedge of a stair tower cutting down through layers of the spiral and rising well above it so that the sharp profile of the spike could be seen against the sky. The wedge spiked the rotunda the way a collector's pin might fix a beetle without compromising its form. The inflected receiver is replaced with a wall that imposes a different kind of attachment with a geometry determined by the box, not by the complexities of Wright's plan, an accidental collision of conflicting forms in which the new absorbs the old. The rotunda, the remarkable flying form that makes the work of art, loses a critical part of its autonomy and becomes dependent on the

144

new box—a remarkable dependency but a dependency nonetheless.

The addition causes a comparable compromise inside. Until the new space was added, the interior was wholly controlled by the rotunda's great spiral ramp, conceded to be difficult for the display of art but central to the peculiar identity of the museum. With occasional recesses to relieve its descent, the ramp is powerfully continuous, the ceiling curving down with the floor, with any turn off it only an incident in the relentless progress of its inescapable slope. The new box grafts onto the ramp a stack of conventional rectangular galleries, attached by steps and ramps to reconcile their flat floors with the sloped rotunda. This stack of galleries is no small hiccup; it changes the experience by inserting a contrasting kind of space into the official route through the museum. The insert can be ignored, but it sets up a conflict about the museum's intentions and a real awkwardness when the invitation to leave the ramp for the new galleries is accepted and the experiences are mixed. The addition thus has a double impact: while the new box tames the rotunda outside, its galleries undermine the effect of its interior ramp. The result is a pretentious failure of curatorship, of understanding and respect, on the part of an owner who should have known better.

WASHINGTON COURT, GREENWICH VILLAGE

Additions frequently affect groups of works that together create identifiable protected districts. The site for the Washington Court apartments on the Avenue of the Americas in New York City was a vacant lot at the end of a block characteristic of the Greenwich Village Historic District. The district is the consistent, dense, eclectic product of the explorations in New York of urban middle-class domestic architecture in the 150 years before

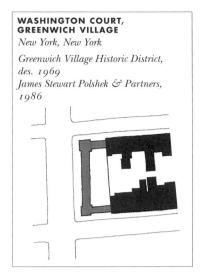

WASHINGTON COURT, GREENWICH VILLAGE
New York, New York
Greenwich Village Historic District, des. 1969
James Stewart Polshek & Partners, 1986

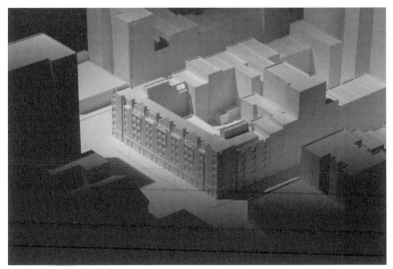

3-133

3-133. James Stewart Polshek & Partners' proposal fits into the form of the Village

3-134

3-135

3-134. The design's somewhat bohemian ideas about housing

3-135. Washington Court in the Village

World War II. Consisting predominantly of four-, five-, and six-story rowhouses with higher and larger lofts and apartment buildings mixed in, the varied streetscapes, house fronts, and frequent skylights of the Village manifest in a wide range of materials, forms, shapes, and styles a relaxed, expressive license evoking radicals and artists that once made it New York's bohemia.

The Washington Court site is large for the Village and exposed by the width of the Avenue of the Americas. Its zoning called for what could have been a catastrophic high-rise but left a loophole for a low building that would fill the site and maintain a street wall consistent with most Village streets. The architects, James Stewart Polshek & Partners, used the loophole to wrap a solid body of apartments along the perimeter of the site around a central court, maintaining the cornice height of the adjacent buildings (fig. 3-133). The façade stacks a relatively plain middle on a base of storefronts and under an eclectic attic top of mansards, skylights, and chimneys (fig. 3-134). Anchored by two square, symmetrical towers on the avenue, the façade displays windows reflecting two-story apartments inside—new versions of the brownstone studios of the 1920s that are the dream of many a New Yorker—grouped in an overall rhythm reminiscent of the front light courts of early New York multiple dwellings (fig. 3-135). The towers suggest early-twentieth-century radical Viennese workers' housing like the Karl Marx Hof. Within this larger order the windows have a rhythm of their own, helped to be both odd and interesting by small but effective changes of plane, patterns of brick, and embellishments of tile.

The result is an original work that revels in the ideas protected in the Village. It is right in its shape and scale, various and unconventional in its decoration, and quietly but firmly attached directly to the Village's radical bohemia.

SEAMEN'S CHURCH INSTITUTE AND 250 WATER STREET, SOUTH STREET SEAPORT

The South Street Seaport Historic District is the surviving shreds of a very early nineteenth-century waterfront commercial district just south of the Brooklyn Bridge in Manhattan (fig. 3-136). Despite many holes caused by collapse and demolition, the district still implies a consistent formal figure at the size and height set by its oldest small three-, four-, and five-story brick gabled lofts—some with their lift-wheels still in place, and their slightly larger successor warehouses faced in granite. The experience of the original stock has a rugged, preindustrial urbanity tied to the sea by views of the East River and the sailing vessels of the district's Seaport Museum—and by the smell of the Fulton Fish Market.

Since its founding in the 1960s, the seaport has represented a laboratory for preservation techniques. It has tested by the evolving lights of at least forty years of thought on the subject everything from the best way to establish the identity of the thing to be preserved to the largest and most complex financial transactions to make it worth doing so. Restoring the seaport's most important group of buildings, Schermerhorn Row, Jan Hird Pokorny refused to "restore it back" to one hypothetical early state, protecting modifications that were important evidences of the passage of time. Ben Thompson Associates adopted a historicist expression for the new, focal food market, tying the district's future to tourists' apparent preferences for comfortable imagery. Beyer Blinder Belle's design for a bogus old cast-iron building to replace a stolen demountable real one raised complex questions about authenticity. (A heroic public act of simulation by the city of New York maintains the Fulton Fish Market as a maritime commercial presence in the dis-

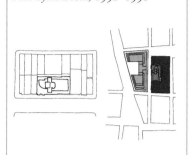

SEAMEN'S CHURCH INSTITUTE AND 250 WATER STREET, SOUTH STREET SEAPORT
New York, New York

South Street Seaport Historic District, des. 1977
James Stewart Polshek & Partners, 1992
Platt Byard Dovell, 1992–1998

3-136. South Street when it was a real seaport

3-136

3-137

3-138

3-137. *Ships of the Seaport Museum, Schermerhorn Row, and a monster office building that supports the South Street Seaport*

3-138. *James Stewart Polshek & Partners' Seamen's Church Institute in its Seaport Historic District block*

trict with fish trucked in from the Bronx!) A good example was set for respectful conversions within the district in Raphael Vignoly's modification of the Beekman Hospital for apartments. A ghastly example was set by the undifferentiated gray horror of the tower built with seaport air rights that looms over Schermerhorn Row (fig. 3-137).

The Seaport was sustained by new construction that kept the old buildings parts of an urban district, not just pieces in a museum. James Stewart Polshek & Partners 1992 Seamen's Church Institute is the most important of the new buildings, the end of the perigrinations of an old New York maritime institution and possibly the best building built in Manhattan since the late 1960s (fig. 3-138). Its site is in the middle of a block, between one of the district's best old buildings and an anonymous, low garage. The design benefits from a complex and interesting institutional program including a chapel, a museum, offices, reception spaces, and bedrooms, all of which are made to enter into the building's expression. The building stays within the size range of district buildings, exploiting the differences in their conventions for the expression of their street fronts and the attics above. The building incorporates the historic building, the height of the new flat, rectangular brick and granite façade matching a variety of set-back galleries and curved enclosing forms in white metal in the attic zone above. The vertical focus of the façade works up from the street entry, with its metal canopy, past special windows in the middle section above it to the bell and flagpole at the apex. The proportions and rhythm of windows across the façade are a version of the standard rhythm of the windows of the old warehouses. The expression of the whole makes clear but sophisticated connections with maritime design ideas, from the rounded corners of the steel windows of the main façade to the funnel and decks of the attic above (fig. 3-

139). The effect of the whole is strong, interesting, original, and completely convincing as a respectful celebration of the district's ideas about preindustrial maritime commerce.

A trapezoidal 46,000-square-foot vacant parking lot across the street from the Seamen's Institute, 250 Water Street presented a design challenge of a whole different order of complexity. The very large site was understandably coveted by its owner and the city for a valuable, taxpaying building. Five architects, including Ulrich Franzen, Jan Hird Pokorny, and Richard Roth, had proposed designs that were rejected by the Landmarks Preservation because they would be different and alien, and dominate and overwhelm the district. Proposals for the site repeatedly stirred violent opposition from neighbors both inside and outside the district.

The proposal approved in 1991 was for office development (fig. 3-140). It took advantage of the size of the site to produce the largest possible floors and hence the lowest possible building. It started by filling in the whole block at the scale of the district, as if to complete its irregular carpet of small three-, four-, and five-story buildings. Then, at the height of the district attic, the design's attic zone was set back irregularly through a transition zone to a core of floors that continued to step back to the top of the building. Like the institute across the street, the base was closely derived from district street walls in brick and granite with windows and a rhythm and detail like old district buildings. Above the base the expression became increasingly more abstract as it set back through intermediate floors of precast concrete to the core floors clad in a contemporary curtain wall as if to draw out and expose a more radical truth beneath the familiar base. The familiar and the abstract interlocked at the entry, where the contempory metal and glass come all the way down to the old street.

3-139

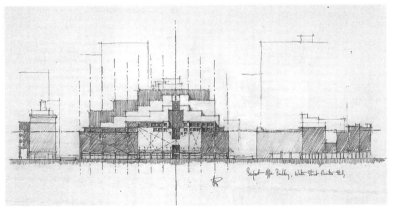

3-140

3-139. The Institute's version of the Seaport's ideas about maritime architecture

3-140. A design that settles a large office building into the Seaport at 250 Water Street

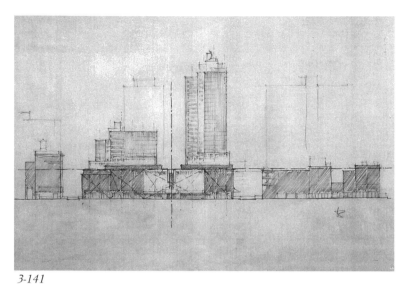

3-141

3-141. *Design for a tall residential building on the same site*

Because the lot was irregular, the resulting form was also highly irregular, an expression of almost continuous transition from the base to the top. The mass was shaped so that the highest point was pulled away from the narrow end on Beekman Street and piled up at the wide north end on Peck Slip. Important to the success of the form was what it was not: a box, a tower, a slab, or even a mixture of standard building forms. Avoiding contrasts of type, it offered instead a complex surface and profile variegated like the district. The whole emerged out of the district like a big hill by the seashore. No longer alien or overwhelming, it offered the district distinct, strong, benign back up for its form.

The Commission approved the project after strenuous review. The project was just as big volumetrically as its unsuccessful predecessors but its character had changed from hostile to something that honored and supported the district. Shortly after the approval, the market for office space in lower Manhattan collapsed and the project languished. When the project returned in 1996 it was a residential project and a different design problem. Unlike the office project, the residential project couldn't be a low lump. To be efficient and marketable, it had instead to be tall and thin. The new design takes the same approach, disposing its program in the same proportions on the site and building a varied, evolving expression up from a base fitted to the district to a finely clad contemporary core set back above. The core above is broken into two related but dissimilar higher forms, one relatively low and predominantly horizontal and one distinctly vertical and tall, with a substantial opening in the middle returning almost to the ground at the entry. Instead of one low hill, the design is now a three-part composition of crags that manages the impact of its size and height by the variety and refinement of its parts, the slenderness of its tallest portion, and the delicacy, balance, and integrity of the composition itself (fig. 3-141). The proposal shared with its successful predecessor a certain strangeness: it is not really like anything anyone has seen before. Tied the same way into the district but going up quite differently into the sky, the support it provides the Seaport was now more sophisticated, but, ideally, no less benign.

Adding Over

Major additions on top of historic buildings start with a handicap. The buildings underneath are necessarily subordinate, as in the Boston Custom House and the New York Merchants' Exchange. Overcoming this handicap is not easy; all of the examples discussed here failed. But each of them is instructive in its failure about the principle at work.

WHITNEY MUSEUM OF AMERICAN ART

Marcel Breuer's 1966 Whitney Museum in New York (fig. 3-142) is a pure example of the Bauhaus interest in small wooden blocks—cubes, oblongs, and other shapes to be fondled in the hand and arranged with the fingertips—as instruments for understanding and composing architectural form. But for the trapezoidal windows cut into its skin, Breuer's museum could have been one of these blocks blown up, solid, gray, and impenetrable, set up for effect on its small end. The effect is considerable at full size, the solitary museum with its gravity-defying stepped overhang a disquieting proclamation of otherness amid the shops, brownstones, and apartments of New York's Upper East Side Historic District.

When the Whitney commissioned Michael Graves to expand its obdurate block in 1985 he ended its solitude, building it into a composition of comparable new objects. To the south a new blocklike object at roughly

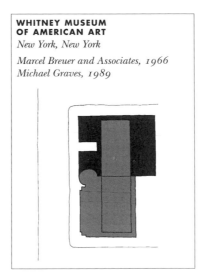

WHITNEY MUSEUM
OF AMERICAN ART
New York, New York

Marcel Breuer and Associates, 1966
Michael Graves, 1989

3-142

3-142. Marcel Breuer's severe Bauhaus block for the Whitney Museum with the wall abstracting it from its neighbors

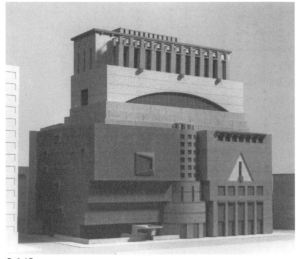

3-143

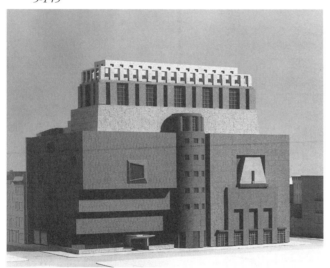

3-144

3-145

the same scale balanced the original, with a tapered, semicylindrical stair tower in between. A long, rectangular third object laid over them on its side tied them together with a large, arched window that reinforced the idea of connection. The combination of the new and the old was vastly larger than the original. The parts were all strongly articulated and now highly colored, as if to develop from what Breuer had started toward something a little less grim (fig. 3-143).

Graves's start was promising. Taking off from the original's essential Bauhaus objectness, he made a point of it, combining the original with more objects, ending its isolation and making it participate, however reluctantly, with new mates. As in much of Graves's work, there was a question of scale; it was hard to know how big anything was supposed to be. In drawings his buildings often seem comically small, like piles of colorful toys. The Whitney too was made to seem like a toy, a gray, grumpy, reluctant old boy at the bottom of a jolly game of colorful new lumps, a game that it might have set in motion but no longer controlled.

Subject to regulation in the historic district, Graves's proposal was denounced as big and aggressive and progressively reduced in size, complexity, and character (fig. 3-144). The proposal got drabber and drabber and its components less objectlike, which allowed Breuer, to a degree, to reassume command as the principal object in a combined work of ever-decreasing interest (fig. 3-145). Reaction to the abandonment of the project depended in part on the degree of affection for the original; if Breuer's Whitney always seemed rather pompous, one might not have minded seeing it in a combination in which it had to work a bit, which prodded it to cheer up. But taking the Whitney with all the high seriousness with which it was originally offered, and accepting its significance as one of the principal and most public built representa-

152

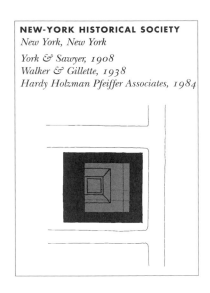

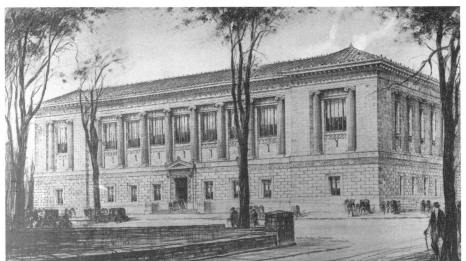

3-146

tives of the ideas of its school, the new composition at its freshest did much to demean, not celebrate it. Even as the addition was dumbed down, Breuer never quite got out from under the impact of what would have been an unworthy new group of neighboring forms.

NEW-YORK HISTORICAL SOCIETY

The current home of the New-York Historical Society was conceived by York & Sawyer in 1908 as a single building occupying an entire block front facing Central Park. Two strong corner pavilions were to have joined a heroic colonnade under a shallow pitched tile roof in what is now the Central Park West Historic District (fig. 3-146). The society first built and for some thirty years lived in just the central colonnaded gallery (fig. 3-147). The end pavilions were finished by Walker & Gillette in the late 1930s in a stripped version of the original classical design (fig. 3-148). The result was not a great building but good enough to become a designated landmark.

Hardy Holzman Pfeiffer Associates' 1984 proposal to expand the building with a superimposed residential tower faced a dou-

3-147

3-148

3-146. York & Sawyer's original design for the New-York Historical Society

3-147. The portion the Society first built

3-148. Walker and Gillette's design for its completion

3-149

3-150

3-151

3-149. Hardy Holzman Pfeiffer Associates' proposed massing

3-150. The scenographic elevation

3-151. A model of the tower in the Central Park West Historic District

ble hurdle—to make a proper contribution to the historic district as well as to the individual landmark. The design piled up chunks of building on the base provided by the Historical Society, like a realized Byzantine painting of a hill town. Viewed straight on from the park, the elevation was straight and symmetrical over the symmetrical façade of the society (fig. 3-149). Viewed askance it was asymmetrical, as if the tower were twisting into the lower adjacent buildings even as it stood out like a post to mark its important corner in the district (fig. 3-150). The façades were graphically subdivided in units—for example, groupings of windows with related pediments or implied arcades—related to comparable units of the old building but with their proportions successively altered in the transition of the building from its horizontal base into the vertical tower. The expression was adapted from decorative ideas present in the old building but developed with the strength, abstraction, and flatness of scene-painting characteristic of Hardy Holzman Pfeiffer's work.

The proposal was found appropriate to the district; the animated and complex tower seemed acceptable in the context of the neighborhood and of its comparably decorated towers (fig. 3-151) but not to the old building. The central tapered tower firmly fixed the old building like the ground under a rocket. The energetic form and strongly ornamented surfaces of the tower made the new building substantially the most magnetic part of the composition. At the same time, while not mocking, the friendly, scenographic takeoff of the old building's decoration undercut its seriousness, a deflation hard for the old building to survive. Where other asymmetrical, plainer, more deferential proposals might have kept the protected building the object of the new combination, this one took command, sat on it, and put it down.

METROPOLITAN CLUB

A contemporary proposal for the landmark Metropolitan Club on the other side of Central Park failed for similar reasons. The club is a large 1894 Renaissance Revival light-buff palazzo by McKim, Mead & White that stands out on its corner of Fifth Avenue with all the self-importance of its founders, J. P. Morgan and his friends (fig. 3-152). Elegantly planned to make its entire frontage on Central Park available for club rooms, the building offers a relatively tall, smooth marble front with well-formed, regular windows resting on a solid base and topped by a projecting cornice strong enough to hold it all together.

In a temporary shortage of tycoons in 1986, the club sought to raise revenue by adding apartments. James Stewart Polshek & Partners designed a shaft of them over a back corner and a wing of the landmark going virtually straight up against the adjacent Pierre Hotel (fig. 3-153). The design tried to avoid treating the landmark as a base but rather to work the new and old together in a new composition. The new tower derived its expression from the old building's formal and decorative conventions in a manner more straightforward and obviously dutiful than Hardy's scenographic abstractions at the Historical Society. Tied into the porte-cochere behind the old building, the new shaft had a relatively plain middle and ended in an ornate top with pilasters and a hefty cornice like the great cornice of the landmark.

It is in this development of the shaft, particularly in the adoption of the cornice as its most prominent feature, that the composition seems to get in trouble (fig. 3-154). Early tall buildings indeed used cornices to complete their forms, drawing a line against the sky to tie down the composition below. McKim, Mead & White themselves stretched the possibilities of a device that

METROPOLITAN CLUB
New York, New York

McKim, Mead & White, 1894
James Stewart Polshek & Partners, 1987

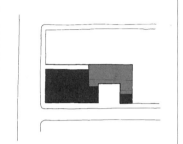

3-152. McKim, Mead & White's Metropolitan Club

3-153. James Stewart Polshek & Partners' proposed addition rises up against the Hotel Pierre

3-154. The tower with its own cornice

3-152

3-153

3-154

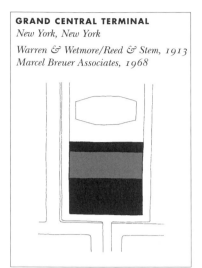

GRAND CENTRAL TERMINAL
New York, New York

Warren & Wetmore/Reed & Stem, 1913
Marcel Breuer Associates, 1968

3-155

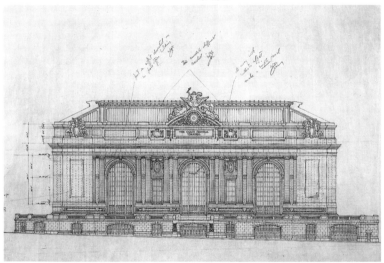

3-156

3-157

3-158

worked at the Metropolitan Club and the University Club but began not to work on buildings as tall as the Pennsylvania Hotel. The adoption of the cornice for the new tower spoke to that convention as well as making a direct connection with the cornice below, from which it was obviously and closely derived.

The choice of the cornice was made against the background of the obvious alternative held out by the Pierre Hotel, the taller shaft against which the new tower rose. The elaborate top of the Pierre offered a different terminal event for its shaft, one which would taper and dissolve into the sky, its version of the breakthrough alternative that helped great skyscrapers use slenderness to make a delight out of their size. Between the club's projecting cornice and the tapering finial of the Pierre, the mid-size new tower had a range of choices for its own termination. Within this range the importance of the original cornice to the identity of the landmark argued for a choice other than the one that was made. With the closely comparable new cornice in place above it, the old building lost the strength it enjoyed as the sole possessor of a remarkable feature and had to compete for attention with the prominent derivative form—an unnecessary competition with itself. The choice was subtle but not hard. A different resolution of the new shaft might have left Morgan's club, in all its self-importance, a little more comfortably in charge.

GRAND CENTRAL TERMINAL

Marcel Breuer's design for an office tower over Grand Central Terminal is the fundamental example of the issues of superimposition and the one on which American laws of preservation rest.

Warren & Wetmore's terminal building is one of America's finest and most famous Beaux-Arts buildings and one of New York

City's first official landmarks (fig. 3-155). It is important as a railroad station and as one of the icons of New York's identity (fig. 3-156). With the beckoning Miss Liberty and the overachieving Empire State Building, Grand Central's extraordinary concourse is the awesome built moment of arrival in New York, the nation's celebrated place of personal fulfillment (see page 12).

The terminal was conceived as a site for development, the centerpiece of Terminal City (fig. 3-157). Early proposals showed possible façades for buildings over the terminal that drew their expression from the conventions of the terminal itself, notably, a deferential Beaux-Arts design that might be attributed to Warren & Wetmore. Later proposals generally demolished the terminal (fig. 3-158) to expand its functional and financial contribution.

At the time of the Breuer proposal, the terminal could best be seen from Park Avenue on the south. Warren and Wetmore's principal façade, with its famous Mercury clock, filled the bottom of a large void in the surrounding fabric of New York, a void defined by hotels and office buildings, including Pietro Belluschi's sixty-story Pan Am building over the terminal to the north (fig. 3-159).

Breuer's design filled the void with a fine example of ideas about office-tower design then in good currency, a thin, tall, rectangular block stood on end, its principal façade aligned with the terminal's façade below (fig. 3-160). Mechanical floors divided the new tower in three unequal portions with a capital in the large mechanical room behind louvers at the top. The form was a version of the Seagram Building archetype, somewhat flattened and given a masonry skin. It rose on piers with the shadow of a reveal between itself and the terminal that now became its ornate and different Beaux-Arts base. The railroad had Breuer design Machiavellian alternatives: one that would

3-159

3-160

3-155. Grand Central Terminal: the iconic façade of New York

3-156. The façade as drawn

3-157. The future according to Reed & Stem

3-158. I. M. Pei's 1956 proposed replacement for Grand Central

3-159. The setting for Marcel Breuer's tower addition

3-160. Breuer's proposal in its setting

save the great arrival concourse and demolish the exterior, and one that would save the exterior and do in the arrival concourse. The best of the schemes saved the concourse and the façades, balancing the new office building over the terminal's waiting room. The New York City Landmarks Preservation Commission found the proposal inappropriate, saying that the design seemed an aesthetic joke, one that reduced the terminal to the status of a curiosity.

While Breuer might have preferred to modernize the terminal completely by taking it down, he almost certainly did not intend to mock it. His plain, stone-clad Bauhaus block was a characteristically serious expression of commercial modernism. It accurately reflected the railroad's banal office program but also gave it a monumentality to go with the terminal. The modernist assumption he reflected—that it would be absurd to apply Beaux-Arts expressive devices to large quantities of fungible twentieth-century office space—was an abiding truth. The reveal he provided between the two expressions was, by the lights of his architecture, an adequate device to honor differences and bring out the significance of almost any juxtaposition.

The problem had to do with the fact that the tower was over the terminal. The terminal was no longer in sole command of its site. Now it had to work out its meaning in combination with something very large and very different which it was underneath. The superimposition of the confident new tower gave it a polemical edge, an apparent claim of superiority for its newness and a corresponding condescension to the old terminal below. The modern tower was clearly over the terminal, indeed borne forward in triumph by it like a locomotive.

The rejection of the proposal—the struggle and ultimately successful revolt of the old against the assumed superiority of the new—was a turning point in the history of the protection of the public worth of architectural expression and the greatest affirmation to date of its importance. With the demolition of Pennsylvania Station, the bloom was off the new. Respect for old architecture was simultaneously stiffening. The villain of the conflict was speculative office development, expressed like the railroad's proposal in the architecture of commercial modernism. From its point of view, Breuer's design served up the issues with great force and clarity at just the wrong time.

The matter was not easy one for the Landmarks Preservation Commission. Since the concourse was to survive, it came down exclusively to the expressive issues presented by the combined exterior. The Commission was sensitive about its jurisdiction from a constitutional point of view and reluctant to engage a bankrupt and litigious owner who had nothing to lose politically.

The Commission nevertheless dug in its heels and was upheld by the United States Supreme Court in 1978 after years of litigation. Breuer's proposal went into the file as a great instructive lesson. The enduring void above the terminal itself became a landmark in a turn in the national political tide and in the nation's attitudes toward the impacts of architecture on architecture.

Treating preservation cases as special cases in the evaluation of larger building types—as combined works subject to a special rule for the relative importance of the parts combined—offers a number of advantages. The evaluation of preservation cases starts with the obvious part of the protected work, its expression, not what it turns out to be as a matter of fact. The issue, that is, is not whether the work is original or Mission-style or rented to Dvorak or slept in by Washington, matters of fact known or learned from labels, but of the meaning that the protected condition immediately conveys to any affected observer as a work of art, in its state before and after its expression has been affected by the proposed new work. This emphasis on the effects of expression acknowledges the aesthetic foundation underneath all forms of curatorship—namely, that it is worth saving the thing itself rather than saving a book about the thing—so that the thing can make its own meaning available as intended, through experience, to anyone.

The emphasis on expression and on the meaning it conveys has the related advantage of a certain flexibility, of allowing room to move. Thus, the emphasis is not on the protection of expression per se but on the protection of the meaning conveyed by expression, for which the protection of the entire expression may or may not be required. It responds among other things to the fact that the protected work will have an internal hierarchy of its own, that parts of it will be more important than others to the projection of its protected meaning. It acknowledges, too, the possibility that an officially valued meaning may in fact be enhanced by a change in its expressive context. Within its range of movement, the inescapable and often intensely beneficial impacts of architecture on architecture can be cheerfully accommodated.

As part of a framework for legal decision making, this understanding of expression and meaning responds to the need to approach judgment with a degree of objectivity. It supposes and takes advantage of the inherent objectivity of both expression and architectural meaning, that a work worthy of protection will have roughly the same impact on different observers equally informed, observant, and well disposed, and they will draw roughly the same lessons from it. The lessons and conclusions observers draw from a building may vary but they will all come from the same acknowledged basic architectural proposition. The test takes advantage as well of the inherent objectivity in the connections between expressive means and the meanings they generate, which will allow only a reasonable range of difference in the effects that must be protected for the observer to get from one to the other.

The focus on expression and meaning in this approach is also, importantly, a proposition in two parts. Like the old maxim about rules and their reasons, it provides a structure for argument. It serves the purposes of the public regulatory context by giving it a way to proceed by presentation, argument, and the application of an accessible test, not simply by reference to the passions of factions or the likes and dislikes of cognoscenti. It also serves the purposes of those dealing with the regulatory context and needing to make a case for their proposals; it structures their argument and gives it a goal.

The test for success, finally, builds upon the notion of hierarchy that organizes works of art generally and uses it to help determine what can and what should not be done to the old work and whether in the new combined work preservation has been achieved. The test turns on an analysis that affected observers and regulators should be able to make, with a reasonable degree of objectivity and with reasonably predictable results, satisfying themselves by a relatively straightforward assessment of relative importance that the protected meaning has been provided the understanding, display, and support it deserves.

4-1. The architecture of additions: Foster, Casson, and Stirling collaborate at Cambridge University

4 Combined Works and Contemporary Expression: The Architecture of Additions at the End of the Twentieth Century

Focusing preservation on issues of expression and meaning in combined works has the cardinal virtue of attaching preservation to its subject matter at the highest level—the contribution of the art of architecture to the understanding of the human condition. Preservation is thus acknowledged as an act of great importance, as part of the public curatorship by which we preserve not just artifacts but understandings that give us the opportunity to live as we should. Just as we build and visit art museums, we take in protected architecture for its reminders of what the creative mind from time to time can do.

Attaching preservation to architecture this way also turns it from a retentive discipline to an aspect of a creative paradigm, the architecture of additions. The central act of preservation, in this view, is the creation of successful combined works through the collaboration of creative minds across time (fig. 4-1). The later mind acts as if the work of its predecessor were riches not just to be protected but to be redeveloped as part of a combined expression of their common business. Thus Bernini took up the invitation of Michelangelo's dome and added his extraordinary collector to organize and set in motion the process towards its reward. Wren brought the exalted domesticity of Jones's Queen's House in and out of the middle of his monumental hospital, attaching the crown to the care, not just the destruction, of sailors. And Scarpa extracted from the fortress of the Castelvecchio a demonstration of the resistance its art ultimately seeks to overcome, of death itself.

The same creative paradigm drives even the strictest acts of building conservation, as when an engineer like Robert Silman devises stringy metal plates to replace the end-nailed two-by-fours of Frank Lloyd Wright's Wingspread. And it continues to drive the creation of major combined works that use old architecture in their exploration of con-

4-2

temporary expressive agendas, as a brief review of four loose categories of current works can show.

The Architecture of Imitation

If the great expressive tool of modernism was abstraction, reactions against modernism favored the literal use of old expressive conventions brought back like the pictorial reality of representational art. Efforts to recover these conventions fit with a conservative search for reassurance in the old and an appeal to notions that a better and less fallible humanity could somehow be recovered if you scratched off change. The "representational" buildings of Robert A. M. Stern—architect of the Norman Rockwell Museum (fig. 4-2) among other buildings—developed and advocated old conventions as if they represented a recoverable expressive orthodoxy. Conventions could be brought back whole or in pieces like the fragments hung on postmodern buildings to soften them up and make them lovable. References to old conventions could come back as welcome signs as they did on road-

4-2. Robert A. M. Stern's Norman Rockwell Museum in Stockbridge, Massachusetts

4-3

4-4

4-3. Kevin Roche imperceptibly extends the High Gothic of New York's Jewish Museum

4-4. The Parthenon of imitation architecture, the Governor's Palace, Colonial Williamsburg

side commercial buildings of all shapes and sizes across the nation.

The revival of old conventions had obvious connections with back-to-basics rhetoric, as if the modern part of the twentieth century were a forgettable aberration. It offered, however, special risks as a source of expression for combined work, notably in the confusion it engendered as to what was truly old architecture and what was imitation. The confusion could be relatively harmless, as in Kevin Roche's imperceptible addition to the Jewish Museum (fig. 4-3). There wasn't much of the imitation and its complete lack of expressive independence represented an architectural subordination acceptable the way Asplund's classical extrusion of the Göteborg Courthouse might have been acceptable had its genius architect not come up with something better. The confusion, however, could add significantly to the damage done by additions that were inappropriate to begin with. The reconstructions at Williamburg (fig. 4-4) thus started out badly by burying the lesson the surviving foundations could have evoked about American transience. To the extent they claimed to be equivalents of the real lost buildings, the reconstructions added to the injury by minimizing the difference that made the real thing worth honoring in the first place.

This undermining by imitation had its effects even in imitations that were not so literal, where continued developments of old expressive conventions likewise masked the reality of change. Representational architecture became pervasive, however, given its superficial compatibility with old buildings and the great commercial value of its recall of the past. Products themed with historical pieces—cupolas on Howard Johnson's or half-timbers on affordable housing—were reassuring and sold well. Levittown's colonial designs helped veterans anticipate feeling comfortable and at home, and hence eager to buy. Disney's Celebration and the suburbs of the New Urbanism refined and amplified the same comforting devices to reach bigger spenders. The pleasures of similar evocations of a mythic past underlay architectural entertainments like New York New York, in Las Vegas (fig. 4-5).

The commercial value of imitations led both to their proliferation and to an intensification of the confusion from which they sought to benefit. The Forty-second Street project, a major investment in commercial entertainment buildings in Manhattan, for example, seeks to induce spending with a gaudy atmosphere derived from New York's early-twentieth-century theatrical past (fig. 4-6). To its great credit, the public part of the development restores a significant number of valuable old theaters. In other parts of it, however, commercial participants use pieces of the real in a way that is more subversive, taking bits of the old, dismantling, inflating, and reattaching them to new structures as if the new were the old. If you don't know better—in the absence of a large, flashing warning—you are meant to loosen your purse at the pull of the imitation's claim to authenticity.

The success of imitation architecture says many things about the society that welcomes it—notably, the society's discomfort with reality and the lengths to which it will go to escape it. Imitation architecture is the architecture of a society that doesn't want to know the difference between the imitation and the real. To the extent the imitation succeeds in obscuring the difference, it dishonors the past that it profits from.

4-5

4-6

4-5. New York New York in Las Vegas

4-6. The reality of New York's Forty-second Street substantially enhanced

Architecture in the Shape of Things

In the middle of the twentieth century a number of architects took advantage of available wealth and technical resources to make buildings in shapes that were embodiments

163

4-7

4-8

4-9

4-10

4-7. Eero Saarinen's TWA terminal at Kennedy Airport in New York

4-8. Santiago Calatrava tries something similar for the French Railways' new TGV station at Lyon

4-9. Rem Koolhaas's big "L" for the Credit Lyonnais at Eurolille in Lille

4-10. Koolhaas's embodiment of twentieth-century consumption at Lille Expo

of the meanings they sought to express, like birds in flight. In the hands of an artist like Eero Saarinen, the results could be breathtaking (fig. 4-7). In lesser hands, their ambitious forms survive to remind us of the hubris of an era we have come to envy. In vernacular artifacts like the Long Island farmstand in the shape of a duck celebrated by Robert Venturi, they remind us not to take ourselves too seriously.

In a comparable period of wealth and ambition in the 1980s, architecture in the shape of things came back to serve many of the same purposes—for example, in Santiago Calatrava's TGV station in Lyon, a signpost for the costly ambitions of the French railroads (fig. 4-8). Shaped architecture has also been used to come to grips with, and even to try to lighten, some of the grimmest commercial realities of our times. In Lille, Rem Koolhaas's flaring L-shaped boot makes anonymous offices of the Credit Lyonnais into an unexpected object of interest (fig. 4-9). His strange and powerful assembly of cheap building materials at the nearby convention center elevates the inherent ugliness of large-scale contemporary consumption without the least concealing it (fig. 4-10).

Where shaped architecture meets old buildings in combined works, it raises the opposite issue from the architecture of imitation, not a problem of sameness but the need to exploit or reconcile differences that are obviously vast.

WEXNER CENTER FOR THE VISUAL ARTS

Contemporary theoretical architecture has explored uncertainties found by contemporary philosophy in the meanings of words and in meaning itself. Its contemplation of uncertainty—its search for an architecture for man in the unknown and unknowable—has made a place for the heroic view of architecture in an unheroic world. From an academic base outside a world unlikely in any event to build its designs, it has rewarded adventurous unbuilt work with attention and respect. Pursuing forms to express the condition of man in what it sees as a charged, transient, anguished state, theoretical architecture used the computer to make its proposals visible, credible, and increasingly buildable. Where it has built work, the accommodation of its thought with reality has sometimes been awkward, like the titanic bundles of reinforcing rods necessary to build some of its jagged forms.

Peter Eisenman's Wexner Center (fig. 4-11) is a built representation of theories of its architect, the first popular work of an engaging one-time enfant terrible. Completed in 1990, the Center itself transforms two ordinary limestone academic buildings—Mershon Auditorium (1957) and Weigel Hall (1979)—at the edge of the Ohio State University campus and on one side of a major pedestrian entry into the campus. The principal of the two buildings, the Mershon Auditorium, addresses a major street, presenting its side to the campus entry. Behind the Mershon, the Wexner Center squeezes between it and Weigel and then bursts out onto the paving of the wide pedestrian entry, engaging its traffic and enriching the introduction to the campus.

The Wexner Center does nothing but good for the old buildings, improving their joint attachment to the campus and redeeming their relative banality. Against their background, the Wexner first shows itself off as an appealing aggregate of forms abstracted from reimaginings of an old armory once associated with the site. These forms introduce a series of galleries and a parallel, long, outdoor, white-painted steel walkway forcibly wedged between the old buildings (fig. 4-12). The walkway dramatizes a collision of grids drawn from the city plan. The colliding grids run through the interior of the building shaping its spaces and organizing its decoration down to the smallest detail.

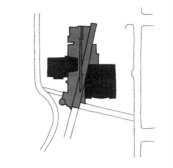

WEXNER CENTER FOR THE VISUAL ARTS
Columbus, Ohio

Mershon Auditorium, 1957
Weigel Hall, 1979
Eisenman/Trott, 1989

4-11. Peter Eisenman's brick and metal Wexner Center enlivens the entry to Ohio State

4-12. The Wexner Center wedged between two existing theaters

4-11

4-12

4-13. *Frank Gehry's "Fred and Gin-*
ger" with the neighbor behind them in
Prague

4-14. *A run of riverfront façades dis-*
solves into Fred and Ginger

The Wexner Center uses its great differ-ence to the advantage of the combination and the context. Where it gives trouble is on its own terms, as it rigorously follows out implications of its collision of grids to gen-erate internal spaces that are difficult to use for anything at all. This demonstration that the theory is archibabble weakens the Cen-ter's case for the arts at the entry to the cam-pus.

FRED AND GINGER

Frank Gehry's sculptural architecture brings out meanings that can be conveyed by shape—movement, for example—some-times doing so abstractly and sometimes dressing its shapes to read as a known objects in motion, like his famous fish. The work explores a range of possibilities, from intu-itively appealing and powerful abstract sculp-tural forms like the Guggenheim in Bilbao to buildings incorporating whole heroic known objects, like the Oldenburg field glasses of Chiat-Day in Venice, California.

Gehry's corner office building on the Vtlava in historic Prague, which has come to be known as "Fred and Ginger," is some-where in the middle of the range. The pro-ject is conceived as an extension of the city's sensuous and athletic old baroque, with its abundant statuary and multiple references to the human body (fig. 4-13). The corner of the building originally sketched by Croatian architect Vladimir Milunic was to be a hero-ic modern nude, a completely naked kary-atid. Gehry abstracts the woman into two cylinders that seem to dance together "Gin-ger" has a 1950s woman's waist and is clad in plates of transparent glass, a combination of finery and nakedness. Underneath, her exposed structure comes down to the side-walk in the multiple steps of a dance turn. "Fred," holding Ginger's waist, is straighter and more opaque, anchoring the pair.

As a plastic evocation of motion, dance,

4-13

4-14

and the human body, the basic scheme seems a wonderful twentieth-century extension of the local baroque. Where it suffers is as it gets literal enough to be tagged with the appellation "Fred and Ginger" (even in a city with long and important associations with film) and then, with a shoddy-seeming skin, hokey windows, and wavy pencil lines of decoration pulled from the neighboring streetscape, flattens itself out into what seems perilously like a billboard about itself (fig. 4-14). Somewhere between a joke and a commentary, "Fred and Ginger" reads like a printed illustration that could ultimately become as annoying as advertising on Prague's remarkable riverfront.

JEWISH WING, BERLIN MUSEUM

Daniel Libeskind's extension of the Berlin Museum to house its Jewish collection dramatizes other possibilities of sculptural architecture. Seen from the sky in its model, the extension combines two different understandings of a line, a buffeted, zig-zag bolt of destruction that houses and incorporates a short straight line for the ghastly destructive progress to the death-camps and the grave (fig. 4-15). The plan is like the conventional U of the comfortable old museum but straightened, stretched, and tortured. Its elevation is the flattest of abstractions next to the conventional old museum façade, stabbed and cut to let in sharp shafts of light. Its slit thin metal skin seems cheap and expendable, worthless like the victims of the Holocaust to their murderers (fig. 4-16). Beside the old museum, the extension constructs the vast pain of the appalling fact it commemorates the way the mannerists built or carved the suffering of saints. The overwhelming power of the addition, its abrupt outgrowth from the ordinariness of the old museum, seems an effective exploitation of the vastness of the difference between them (fig. 4-17).

JEWISH WING, BERLIN MUSEUM
Berlin, Germany

*Philipp Gerlach, 1735
reconstructed 1960s
Daniel Libeskind, 1997*

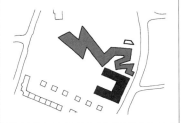

4-15. The model of Daniel Libeskind's Jewish Wing of the Berlin Museum like a terrible bolt of lightning

4-16. The Berlin Museum in the shadow of the Jewish Wing

4-17. The slashed skin of the JewishWing

4-15

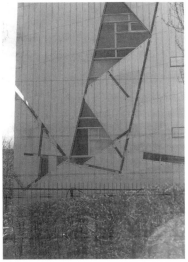

4-16

4-17

**THE BOILERHOUSE,
VICTORIA AND ALBERT MUSEUM**
London, England

*Victoria and Albert Museum, 1857–
Daniel Libeskind, 1998*

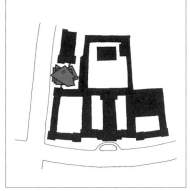

4-18

4-19

4-20

THE BOILERHOUSE, VICTORIA AND ALBERT MUSEUM

At the Victoria and Albert Museum (fig. 4-18), in contrast, Libeskind had a more generalized drama to bring home. The proposed addition known as the Boilerhouse was set in the short last gap in the long perimeter of buildings that house Britain's historic collection of decorative arts (fig. 4-19), twisting the line of the perimeter into a spiral of flat plates over a jagged pile of exhibit spaces (fig. 4-20). The surfaces of the plates were brightly colored and broken up in patterns derived from fractal geometry, as if to suggest a larger mathematical order that might make sense of its form. The novelty of the design was a different, high evocation of the interest in inventive, practical arts that has always driven the museum. Decorative in its bright coloration, the Boilerhouse was disquieting in its view of the cosmos as broken, twisted, and apparently unstable.

Powerful and potentially popular in its novelty—an ecclectic addition to an ecclectic museum—the design departed from the common view of the Victoria and Albert as an attic like the Smithsonian and a repository of work that generally played second fiddle to the major arts. The addition had nothing of the second fiddle in its form. Instead it proposed to bring the V & A into the mainstream with the major arts, indeed to the head of the stream of major arts and of popular, paying art museums. However popular, it did not make the cut for funding under Britain's lottery and remains unrealized.

The Architecture of Appropriateness

The architecture of appropriateness explicitly follows a collaborative approach to design with old buildings. It takes as its starting point the need to understand the expression of the old building and then to express itself in a way that makes clear that understanding and its support for what the old expression says and how it says it. It goes on to make with the old an expression for their common business that is greater and richer than either and that is sometimes importantly redemptive, curing flaws that go along with the positive values of the old building.

JEROME M. GREENE HALL, COLUMBIA LAW SCHOOL

Harrison & Abramovitz's Columbia Law School, famous for its resemblance to a pop-up toaster, was an important representative of the ideas of its time and of the work of an architect who built compromised versions of many of them. Wallace Harrison participated in the realization of the ideas of George Howe and William Lescaze at Rockefeller Center. His shaped buildings, like his fish church in Connecticut or the Oberlin Auditorium, were followers in the class led by Eero Saarinen. His Albany Mall was a Valhalla for conventional modernism.

The Columbia Law School was a stumpy block-and-base combination that oppressed the university and its neighborhood with its coarse modernity. The bridge and raised podium that separated it from the city streets became Columbia's trophy example of a very bad urban planning idea. While beginning to be tolerated as a period piece, the building increasingly poorly represented the contemporary Law School until in 1996 Polshek & Partners's addition substantially reformed and redeemed it (fig. 4-21). The addition of Jerome M. Greene Hall had the happy assignment of tying together the school's split-level entry system and getting the building as a whole to lighten up. It did so by adding an intermediate object to

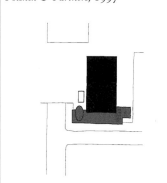

JEROME M. GREENE HALL, COLUMBIA LAW SCHOOL
New York, New York

Harrison & Abramovitz, 1961
Polshek & Partners, 1997

4-18. The tower at the entry of the Victoria and Albert Museum

4-19. Libeskind's Boilerhouse addition among the other buildings of the museum

4-20. The Boilerhouse' fractal view of the universe

4-21

4-21. Polshek & Partners' Jerome M. Greene Hall reestablishes Harrison and Abramovitz's Columbia Law School in the street grid of New York

4-22

4-23

4-24

4-22. *Picking up the axis of the Campus*

4-23. *Going on towards the horizon at the end of the street*

4-24. *With a form derived from Wallace Harrison's United Nations, Greene Hall reinforces the neglected upper entry to the School*

make a lively three-part composition out of the school's two stolid original parts. Its new pavilion was shaped and detailed in ways that picked up, transformed, and made virtues out of elements of the original expression to humanize its representation of the school.

The new pavilion was another simple rectangular block remotely derived from Columbia's original plan. It was made long and elegant and laid on its side in the joint between the heavy original vertical block and the original horizontal base (fig. 4-22). The long rectangle stretched to demonstrate for the first time the connection between the rarely used principal entrance on the podium above and the secondary entrance used by everyone on the street below. The original vertical block was set back and up on its podium to free it from the street, conceived in its time as something dirty, like a slum. The new rectangle pulls its corner back to the street corner, emphasizing the move with its cupola as if to pin the combination into the street grid. On its surfaces the addition translates the original building's stockade of coarse and endless vertical mullions into an assembly of thin, deep horizontal blades shading wide bands of clear glass (fig. 4-23). Wrapping the new object, the endless elegant blades energize the old base and engage it in the street's unusual horizontal expansion away from the Columbia campus, over the cliffs of Morningside Park.

The addition makes other contributions —notably, in the light and life it brings to the street corner through its new clear glass. Next to the original upper entry of the law school, with its huge flying Jacques Lipschitz sculpture, the cupola of the addition recalls Harrison's General Assembly of the United Nations, continuing to try to make a place out of the so-far-unsuccessful upper plaza (fig. 4-24). Without patronizing or demeaning the original, the addition leaves the bulk of the original as the school's principal signifier but represents and reveals on the street the different school of today. It suggests by its development of the original expression that there was more to it than met the eye. The addition helps the school become, by the light of what we have learned since, the work of art it wished to be.

JEWETT ARTS CENTER AND THE DAVIS MUSEUM AND CULTURAL CENTER

Set below Paul Rudolph's masterful Jewett Arts Center at Wellesley College, Rafael Moneo's Davis Museum and Cultural Center (fig. 4-25) makes with the Jewett an unusual three-part combined work that begins with a semicircle of collegiate Gothic gable ends on dormitories rimming the top of a hill. Asked in 1958 to find space for the Jewett opposite the dormitories, Rudolph extended the horizontal plane of the hilltop in three buildings that completed the circle—an auditorium, a connecting entry gallery, and a large rectangular block of offices and workrooms laid on its side (fig. 4-26). Rudolph's buildings picked up and developed the spiky rhythm of the Gothic gable ends, notably in the two rows of delicate angular skylights seen in profile on the roof of the gallery building that made clear the purpose of the buildings as a center for the study of art (fig. 4-27). The expression of Jewett—its columns, steps, and pendant screens—has throughout a remarkable, robust refinement adapted to a women's college, a refinement almost unexpected in a master known later for more brutal work. The Jewett's motif of many quick steps to nowhere, like Carlo Scarpa's exploration of the resistance of the Castelvecchio (see chapter 1), seems to bring home the ultimate seriousness of the study engaged by the Center.

JEWETT ARTS CENTER AND THE DAVIS MUSEUM AND CULTURAL CENTER
Wellesley, Massachusetts
Paul Rudolph, 1958
Rafael Moneo, 1995

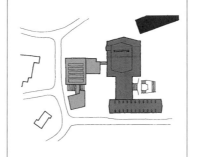

4-25

4-26

4-27

4-25. *Rafael Moneo's Davis Museum at the edge of its plaza below Paul Rudolph's Jewett Arts Center*

4-26. *Up above the end of the oval of gabled dormitories and the Jewett Arts*

Center with the top of the Davis Museum beyond

4-27. *Paul Rudolph's multiple screens and skylights on the Jewett Center*

4-28

Rudolph's extension of the buildings off the hill brings them out over the principal path of circulation to the hilltop. The pedestrian path comes up under the middle of the Jewett's buildings by way of a wide underpass and stair that Rudolph gives a rare amenity and interest. The site for the Davis Museum is below the Jewett at the bottom of the underpass, a substantial vertical distance down from the top of the hill. There Rafael Moneo set the new museum to the side of the ascending approach on a plaza of its own and piled up its galleries to give it a strongly vertical form. Above a glazed entry, its principal side walls are blank brick, plainer than Rudolph's screened glass, and it is crowned with five large saw-tooth skylights, solider, fewer and bigger than Rudolph's but, like his, jagged in profile against the sky (fig. 4-28).

Moneo's vertical development of the Davis Museum ties the enlarged Arts Center into the hill in a new way. The combined work starts with a major new event at the bottom of the steps that reaches up to complete the combined composition above. The hilltop circle begins with the gables of the dormitories, travels around to Rudolph's gallery building and then resolves itself in the profile of the rooftop of the new museum. With the Jewett firmly in the middle, Moneo's museum ends the sequence of the Arts Center with a collection of art and a version of Rudolph's crowning idea. Newly resolute and strong, the Davis's determinate, graspable number of skylights is a definite outcome to the Jewett's pursuit of the study of art.

PALAIS DES BEAUX ARTS

However rich a confection—the stripes of a pastry tube seem almost visible on the multiple peaks of the principal north façade—Bérard and Delmas's 1892 Palais des Beaux Arts in Lille is a strong building that honors a great collection of art with a combination

PALAIS DES BEAUX ARTS
Lille, France

Bérard & Delmas, 1892
Ibos and Vitart, 1997

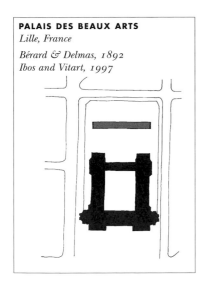

4-29

of delicacy and elegance, a demonstration of the possibilities of Beaux-Arts architecture driven by something other than a thirst for pomp (fig. 4-29). An unfinished U in plan, the museum is less formal in the back, where two fine end pavilions bracket an undecorated arcade, closing off the original central atrium.

Renovating the museum and adding space in and under it in 1997, Ibos and Vitart complete its intended figure with an exceptionally slender and elegant flat glass bar set off a flat court and stretched across the full width of the museum opposite its unfinished end (fig. 4-30), a contemporary presentation piece like the original Beaux-Arts north façade. The principal façade of the addition addresses not the world at large but the museum, calling attention to the old building, not to itself, by beautifully managed reflectivity. To get its particular reflectivity, its flat surface is uniformly stencilled with regular tiny gold bars like holes in a punch card. The glass wall is an uninterrupted plane hung directly in front of an uninterrupted internal void with suspended corridors and a back wall patterned with larger horizontal rectangles, the gold fritted wall and the space behind making a rich pat-

4-29. The set-piece façade of the Palais des Beaux Arts in Lille

4-30. The addition closing the unfinished end of the Palais and retaining its image

4-31. The long façade of the addition defers and almost disappears

4-30

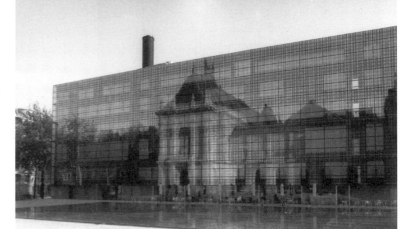

4-31

4-32

4-33

terned mixture of depth and reflectivity. Like the old Beaux-Arts façade, the reflective addition diminishes against the sky—so much so it is hard to find (fig. 4-31). The same reflectivity enforces a relentless deference to the old museum, an unfailing redirection of attention back to it.

The glass establishes a very different balance of absorption and reflectivity on the three outward facing sides of the addition. The glass there is translucent, not reflective, evenly divided by the grid of its structure and enriched by the shadows of stairs and other elements inside (fig. 4-32). From the outside the addition thus reads as a solid object, an effective closure for the original. The object is simpler than the museum but made worthy of it by the simplicity of its form and the inherent elegance of its metal and glass (fig. 4-33). These three sides hold the reflective wall that is the active agent of the connection with the museum, giving the museum control of the addition and completing it with an extraordinary play on its own image, like a work of performance art.

The Architecture of Possibility

The focus of the architecture of possibility is tectonics, the exploration and celebration of the technology of construction and the demonstration in the process of the wonderful possibilities continuing to open to us. Its celebration of technology can excite and amaze. In the best instances, it celebrates a fitness of means to needs, of resources to capacities, rooted in humanism and its admiration of the worth and possibilities of *homo faber*, of individual humans as makers of the devices they need to manage their lives. Tectonic architecture in almost any event works well with old architecture, because it uses the bones of structure and systems common to new and old and makes vivid in the combination the evolution of what they share as buildings and as works of art.

STUDIO NATIONAL DES ARTS CONTEMPORAINS

Bernard Tschumi's design for the Studio National des Arts Contemporains (fig. 4-34), the new French national art school known as Le Fresnoy, outside Lille, and Norman Foster's first design for the Reichstag in Berlin both proposed very large shelters for old buildings as devices to bring out their significance and to set them in the context of the different times in which the old buildings would be put back to work. Foster's relatively minimal roof was at a substantial distance from its awesome artifact, to show it off but also to stand back from it. Tschumi's immensely busy roof tightly embraces the three old entertainment arenas it puts back in service (fig. 4-35). The object of the roof was in fact to weatherproof the old sheds, so that their big "found" spaces could be used with little actual restoration, and to provide a vehicle to service them from above without digging them up or taking them apart. This approach acknowledges and shows off the degree to which the cheap old sheds themselves weren't inherently worth much as buildings. At the same time the sheds gave the new school quirky big spaces very useful for a variety of messy multimedia explorations by graduate students seeking to create high French popular art.

The roof takes off over the first of the old arenas from a wrestler's starting position on the ground (fig. 4-36). As it stretches out over the arenas and the new companion buildings, large openings like stylized clouds in the roof bring light into the old buildings and into the zone between the old buildings and the sky of the new roof. Besides new mechanical systems dropping

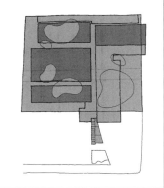

STUDIO NATIONAL DES ARTS CONTEMPORAINS
Tourcoing, France

Arenas Le Fresnoy, 1905
Bernard Tschumi, 1997

4-34. Bernard Tschumi's Studio Nationale visits Tourcoing near Lille

4-35. The old arenas shelter under the Studio's new "sky"

4-34

4-35

4-36. The roof takes off over the combination

4-37. The built domain between the sky and the old arenas

4-38. The two scales of the double stair, one sized for giants and one for us

4-36

4-37

4-38

down from it, the roof provides structure to hang grids and other installations in the old sheds that their own structure could not support. The zone between is cut by the rods, tubes, and columns of these systems with walkways, ramps, and stairs twisted through them like a computer rendering (fig. 4-37), a built version of the "domain" we see through the contemporary looking-glass of the computer screen.

This extraordinary domain is intended and developed for public enjoyment, to be gawked at and played in. Access to it is by a vertiginous split grand staircase, much like the split stair at the entry to the school that once gave access to the entertainments of the arenas. The walkable grillage of the new stair is so porous and airy that going up or down it is like flying or falling—or like stepping through a computer screen. The walkable portion shares the stair with an unwalkable set of colossal risers set at the scale of a realm of giants to whom the addition would be the same in size as the old buildings to us (fig. 4-38). We enter the domain, it seems to say, as the guests of its technology, like children delighted to fear the next violent act of giants on TV, absorbed like them in a virtual world created by technology.

Like Tschumi's famous "follies" at the Parc de la Villette in Paris, Le Fresnoy lands among the scraggly trees of its site like a visitor from another order of imagination, a fantastic device adapted to the subject matter and ambitions of the new school. To serve the twenty-four students of what might be considered a French educational "folie de grandeur," the addition wraps the old arenas in a contemporary entertainment and invites the use of the combination for the exploration of ideas like those the old buildings were built to serve. It celebrates not just the possibilities of contemporary building technology—its extraordinary sheltering shed—but the technology of contemporary creativity—notably the computer—all in a combined work of deeply disturbing charm.

HISTORY AND LAW FACULTIES, CAMBRIDGE UNIVERSITY

Norman Foster's Law Faculty building at Cambridge University directly addresses James Stirling's 1967 History Faculty building, one of the major landmarks of the modern succession. Handsome, complex, and completely original, the History Faculty is a vertical bracket of offices, classrooms, and corridors in tile and glass spiked in place by elevators (fig. 4-39) and embracing a great descending glass greenhouse canopy over its library (fig. 4-40). Its strange and engaging celebration of mechanics and technology—the assemblies of its enclosure, its tracks and cranes, the exposed mechanics of its form—conveyed with red tile and a touch of portent an obvious delight at the creative prospects it opened.

Developed to meet twentieth-century needs at a different scale from earlier university buildings, the History Faculty was built outside the city center next to another large postwar university project, Casson Conder and Partners' 1961 Sidgwick Avenue buildings. A succession of open quadrangles of lecture and reading rooms raised on concrete pilotis over a continuous terrace, Casson's complex was a modernist interpretation of the old college model burdened with a certain high seriousness. Stirling's contrasting piece of visionary ingenuity rose beside one end of Casson's block, the two buildings saying relatively little to each other, fending for themselves on the fringes of the university.

The History Faculty brought with its innovation a series of nearly disastrous technical failures. The ambitions of its greenhouse roof exceeded the performance capacities of 1960s' materials and assemblies, a condition made worse by a postdesign rotation of the building to face the sun more than originally intended. Its sealants failing and its tile falling off, the building would have been

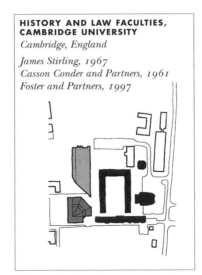

HISTORY AND LAW FACULTIES, CAMBRIDGE UNIVERSITY
Cambridge, England

James Stirling, 1967
Casson Conder and Partners, 1961
Foster and Partners, 1997

4-39

4-40

4-39. The brick towers of James Stirling's restored Cambridge University History Faculty building

4-40. The greenhouse roof of the History Faculty Library framed by the tie rod of Stirling's new neighbor

4-41

4-42

4-43

torn down had not one crusty eminence, out of donnish orneriness and some respect for the design, refused to move out. The History Faculty was accordingly renovated instead and its functional problems relieved. It remained the only truly distinguished twentieth-century building in the university, embarrassed by its own history of difficulties and, but for the self-absorbed Sidgwick Avenue buildings, very much alone.

In 1997 Foster and Partners' Law Faculty ended the isolation of the History Faculty with a powerful form different but descended from Stirling's and almost as strange (fig. 4-41). Sheltering its layers of lawyers with a convex glass roof, anchored on its flat side with a single long slab of offices, the new building lay down in front of Stirling and beside Casson like a high-tech bûche de Noel (fig. 4-42). The end of the bûche was sliced off obliquely—in a curve to save a historic tree. It came to a point in front of the History Faculty, cutting out a place of honor for the combination. The great arched principal façade reflected the pieces and mechanics of Stirling's History Faculty on a plane now infinitely smooth and delicately divided in the rhythm of its blooming curve, its glass as plastic as paint (fig. 4-43). Where Stirling's plates of glass struggled with the sun, Foster's effortlessly controlled it. Where Stirling busily propped everything up against gravity, Foster's enclosure seemed to need to be tied down, the remarkable white tie rod at its apex reaching down as if to complete the combination of its ideas with Stirling's and Casson's with the touch of a wand (see Fig. 4-1).

Foster's descendant building brought with it an echo of the troubles of the History Faculty: the lawyers immediately complained about noise in the great open library. More important, however, it paid homage in its form and its tectonics to Stirling as pioneer and to his building as a historic display of conceptual raw material.

4-44

4-45

4-44. *The Lingotto Fiat Factory, the icon of Italian futurists, in Turin*

4-45. *The ramp to the test track on the roof*

With the Sidgwick Avenue buildings uplifted in the new game and with the big smooth form of the Law Faculty laid out before it, Stirling's valuable pile was now the lead player in a three-part demonstration of the possibilities of adventurous twentieth-century architecture. Its active vertical form and renewed red tile stand out against its neighbors' horizontals and gray tones. Vindicated in its ideas by Foster, the History Faculty seems once again a confident, cheerful, and assertive source of hope.

LINGOTTO CONFERENCE CENTER

The long, thin Fiat plant at Lingotto in Turin, Italy, was a wonder of industrial Europe when it was completed in 1920, raw materials coming in on the ground floor and finished automobiles speeding around a banked rooftop test track, abstracted from the world and shown off in motion against the Alps and the sky (fig. 4-44). The idea of the building was borrowed from America as a model of rational industrial modernism—a bar of rectangular bays repeated and stacked and tied at the ends by coiled ramps up and down from the track (fig. 4-45)—and quickly adopted as

179

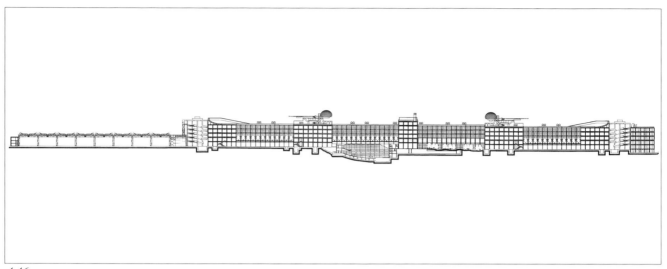

4-46

4-47

4-48

4-46. The vast section of the Lingotto Conference Center with Agnelli Hall in the basement and the conference rooms on the roof

4-47. The new skin at an entry

4-48. Agnelli Hall takes advantage of the void under one of the courts

an icon by Italian Futurists. Lingotto was also very Italian, slender and urbane with a slightly upside down flash of genius in the racetrack on the roof.

When Lingotto became obsolete, the Renzo Piano Building Workshop won a competition for design of its reuse—an exposition and convention center, shopping mall, music library, concert hall, hotel, all slotting into bays in the long frame with lots of room left over (fig. 4-46). Piano's new pieces filled out their bays to the plane of the old surface, glazed in a refined clear glass just distinguishable from the old industrial-glass exterior wall (fig. 4-47). The beautiful shoebox Agnelli Hall (fig. 4-48) fits below-grade under one of the central courts hardly marked on the exterior except by its fire stairs in the piazza. Lifts from the piazza to the mall rise at a slant to deliver shoppers at the arcade around the central courts inside the old frame. In the middle of the long building the elevators of the conference center ascend to the bubble of a ceremonial conference room landed like an ever-so-slightly-alien and insectile helicopter on a bracket over the test track (fig.4-49). Bigger than a car, glowing at night to evoke an unworldly sort of transport, the conference room calls attention to the track and the building like a techy jewel in a rough old lotus.

Of all the competition entries, Piano's did the least to the old building, showing not just restraint but the elegant economy of an ingenious maker of tools to fit the new business into the building. Agnelli Hall, like the Espace de Projection of the IRCAM, is another perfect match of architecture to music. The conference room does just enough to make clear and public the transformation of the car factory into a contemporary device to foster connection, communication, and business. With Piano's inserts and clean detail, the old industrial wonder once again shows off *homo faber* at his admirable work.

4-49

4-49. The first of the Conference Rooms above the old test track.

The Architecture of Additions

The examples in this chapter give a sense of the pleasures of the architecture of additions as a creative paradigm, the rewards of a faithful, insightful, and imaginative undertaking to make for our times the most of the meanings of old buildings. These combined works are all confident buildings, the work of masters in an ancient architectural pursuit. Not one of the additions is afraid of its novelty. Each uses its novelty to explore the opportunities set for it by an existing, resistant body of expressive material. Each treats the old body respectfully, like a collaborator, and works out with it new insights of real value that help us all in the process of making something of our lives today.

Giving preservation place in the architecture of additions helps it embrace its stickiest conceptual problem—that there is in a sense no such thing as "preservation." Every act of preservation is inescapably an act of renewal by the light of a later time, a set of decisions both about what we think something was and about what we want it to be and to say about ourselves today. The value of preservation is only partly in the accuracy and breadth of its understanding of the past. Its value in the end is the presentation the old and the new make together about continuity and difference. The value of the combined work increases, the richer and brighter the light of its novelty.

A place in the architecture of additions also fits preservation into a relatively objective framework for judgments about success and failure. Additions thus are works of art like others, organized and given meaning by their hierarchy. Where a public interest in preservation is involved, that hierarchy should reflect the importance of the thing preserved. Breuer's tower on Grand Central Terminal was hard to beat as an expression of exactly what it was and meant at the time. It also made vivid a painful current conflict between development and preservation. Whatever you thought of one or the other—however well the combination dramatized a truth of urban life—the combination on its own terms did not adequately honor the protected public asset.

ACKNOWLEDGMENTS

The thesis of this study began to become a book after more than thirty years of advocacy and design work with architectural additions, when Robert A. M. Stern invited me to make it a course for all graduating preservation students at the Columbia University Graduate School of Architecture, Planning, and Preservation. The critical enthusiasm of the gifted students in the Preservation Colloquium—more than one hundred and fifty could be called out here by name—was a crucial resource as we tested the thesis and the examples in class over the next five years.

The book developed with initial support from Adolph Placzek and Ulrich Franzen and later with the encouragement of two particularly discerning readers, Robert Kliment and Carter Wiseman. Timothy Seldes set it on the way to publication when he suggested it to Norton. Travel to experience the architecture of its examples was made possible, among other things, by a partial Arnold W. Brunner grant from the New York Chapter of the American Institute of Architects. The labor of assembling photographs was supported by a timely grant from "Furthermore . . .", the J. M. Kaplan Fund Publication Program, and by the work of Natasha Szarkowski. Site plan diagrams were drawn by Marisa Janusz with the help of Frances Puglisi and Victoria Somogyi.

The cheerful Jennifer Wellock did research and the final assembly of photographs and permissions with a rare combination of enthusiasm, insight, and accuracy. Dorothy Miner, legendary Counsel to the New York City Landmarks Preservation Commission, saved the author from more than one error. The whole enterprise came to such good as it has only with the unswerving, critical support of my partners, Charles A. Platt and Ray H. Dovell; my wife, Rosalie Starr Warren; and my editor, Nancy Green, who knows what a book is and what it takes to make one.

PHOTO CREDITS

Cover Dennis Gilbert/VIEW

P-1   Marcel Breuer Papers, Archives of American Art, Smithsonian Institution.

P-2   Courtesy of Hardy Holzman Pfeiffer Associates

I-1   C.O. Buckingham Company Inc.

I-2   Thomas U. Walter Collection, Athenaeum of Philadelphia

I-3   Venturi, Scott Brown and Associates

I-4   Municipal Archives, Department of Records and Information Services, City of New York

I-5   George Pohl/Venturi, Scott Brown and Associates

I-6   Manuscripts Print Collection, Special Collections Department, University of Virginia Library

I-7   Shinkenchiku-sha/The Japan Architect Company

1-2   Courtesy of the Harvard University Archives

1-3   Alinari/Art Resource, NY

1-4   Cicognara VII 664(i)/Foto Biblioteca Apostolica Vaticana

1-5, 1-6, 1-7 Reproduced from John B. Bayley, Letarouilly on Renaissance Rome, Classical America, Architectural Book Publishing Co. (1984)

1-8   Alinari/Art Resource, NY

1-9   Chigi P VII g 17v-18r/Foto Biblioteca Apostolica Vaticana

1-10 All rights reserved, The Metropolitan Museum of Art

1-11, 1-12 Alinari/Art Resource, NY

1-13 National Maritime Museum, London

1-14 The Provost and Fellows of Worcester College Oxford

1-15, 1-16, 1-17 By courtesy of the Trustees of Sir John Soane's Museum

1-18 Colen Campbell, Vitruvius Britannicus

1-21, 1-22, 1-23 Umberto Tomba/Museo di Castelvecchio

1-24, 1-25, 1-26 Klaus Frahm/Contur

1-27, 1-29, 1-30, 1-31 Umberto Tomba/Museo di Castelvecchio

2-1   Foto Marburg/Art Resource, NY

2-3   Martin Charles

2-4   Swedish Museum of Architecture, Stockholm

2-5   Gotesburg Stadsarkiv

2-6, 2-7, 2-8 Swedish Museum of Architecture, Stockholm

2-9   Gotesburg Stadsarkiv

2-10 Swedish Museum of Architecture, Stockholm

2-11, 2-12 Martin Charles

2-13, 2-14, 2-15 Manuscripts and Archives, Yale University Library

INDEX

abstraction, 31, 48, 161

adding over, 151–158

additions. *see* combined works

Allegheny County Courthouse, 84

Allen Memorial Art Museum, 39–43, 135

Altes Museum, 88, 90

American Institute of Architects, 131, 133

Amsterdam, Netherlands, 53–54

angel of built death, 48–49

Anshen + Allen, 115

apartment building, 145–146

appropriateness, 80–84, 168–169

art galleries/museums
    Allen Memorial, 39–43, 135
    Brooklyn Museum of Art, 121–124
    Carré d'Art, 57–60
    Centre Pompidou, 65–67
    Guggenheim Museum, 142–145
    Jewett Arts Center, 171–172
    Kimbell Art Museum, 98, 99–102
    Louvre, 67–70
    National Gallery, 135–136
    Norman Rockwell Museum, 161
    Palais des Beaux Arts, 172–174
    Whitney, 151–153
    Yale University, 36–39

Asplund, Eric Gunnar, 32–36

Baker, Herbert, 103

bank buildings, 49–50, 106–107

baroque design, 18, 48–49

Beaux-Arts design, 110, 112, 156–157
    Palais des Beaux Arts, 172–174

Beekman Hospital, 148

Bel, Philip le, 68

Belcher, John, 95

Belluschi, Pietro, 9, 157

Bérard & Delmas, 172–174

Berlin, Germany, 72–75
    Altes Museum, 88, 90
    Jewish Wing of Berlin Museum, 167

Bernini, Gian Lorenzo, 20–21, 28, 29, 85, 161

Beyer Blinder Belle, 147

Boilerhouse, Victoria and Albert Museum, 168

Boston, Massachusetts, 85, 87–88

Bracken House, 140–141

Bramante, Donato, 18, 19

Breuer, Marcel, 8, 9, 82, 83, 151, 152, 156–158

Brooklyn Museum of Art, 121–124

Brown, A. Page, 137–138

Brunelleschi, 39

brutalism, 124

Budapest, Hungary, 49–50

Buonarotti, Michelangelo, 18, 19, 161

Burr, Aaron, 137

Buttrick White & Burtis, 105

Calatrava, Santiago, 74, 130–131, 164

Cambridge University, 17
    architectural growth, 124
    Downing College, 102–104
    Fitzwilliam College Chapel, 124–126
    History Faculty, 177–179
    Law Faculty, 177–179
    Old Schools, 76
    Saint John's College Library, 124, 126–128
    Senate House, 76

Carrée, Maison, 57–60

Carignano, Palazzo, 140

Carmelite Church, 46–47

Carré d'Art, 57–60, 85

Casson Conder and Partners, 160, 177

Castelvecchio, 15, 18, 161
    museum design, 27–28
    reveals, 27–28
    significance of, 25

Cathedral Church of Sain John the Divine, 128–130

Center for British Art, 39

Central Park, New York
    Dana Center, 98, 105
    Naumberg Bandshell, 91–95

Centre Pompidou, 65–67

Chandler, T. P., 108

Chareau, Pierre, 50–53

Charlottesville, Virginia, 110

Chateau de Marly, 110

Chenavard & Pollet, 70, 71

churches, 46–48. *see also* St. Peter's Church
    Cathedral Church of St. John the Divine, 128–130
    Fitzwilliam College Chapel, 124–126

Clio Hall (Princeton), 137–138

Columbian Exposition, 72, 112
Columbia University, 116–121
  Law School, 169–171
Columbus, Ohio, 164–166
combined works
  act of preservation creation as, 161
  adding over, 151–158
  basis for judgment of, 15, 85, 158–159, 182
  as collaboration, 29
  competition between old and new, 102
  derivations, 50
  of different building types, 124–128
  dilution of original building, 85–91, 102
  extensions, 32
  forms of interaction, 17–18, 32, 84–85
  imitation, 161–163
  masterwork examples, 18, 28–29
  preservation rationale, 182
  successful, 14–15, 75, 91, 182
  tectonic architecture, 174–175
  transformations, 64–65
  use of original plans, 110–125
  wings, 131–151
  see also specific examples
competition with original building, 102
context, 9
  forms of interaction, 17, 84–85
  identity and, 107
Corbusier, Charles-Edouard, Le, 55, 78
courthouse design, 32–36
Cram, Ralph Adams, 128, 130
Credit Lyonnais (Lille), 164
Cullinan, Edward, 126–128
Custom House, Boston, 85, 87–88

Dana Center, 98, 105
Davis Museum and Cultural Center, 171–172
De Bruijn, Pi, 73–74
de Carlo, Giancarlo, 139
derivations, 50–64
dilution of original, 85–91, 102
DOMINO House, 55
Downing College, 102–104

Egeraat, Erick van, 49–50

Egyptian Revival, 108
Eiffel, Gustave, 30
Eiffel tower, 31
Eisenman, Peter, 165–166
environmental movement, 78–79
Equitable Building, 79
extensions
  goals, 32
  modernist examples, 32–50

façades/façadomy, 105
  examples, 106–110
Fairchild Center for Life Sciences, 116–121
Falkestrasse 6, 48–49
Fallingwater, 142
Fitzwilliam College Chapel, 124–126
500 Fifth Avenue, 54–57
Fort Worth, Texas, 99
Foster, Norman, 17, 160, 175
  Cambridge University Law Faculty, 177, 178–179
  Carré d'Art, 57–60
  Reichstag, 72–75
Frankfurt, Germany
  Museum for Pre- and Early History, 43, 46–48
  Museum of Decorative Arts, 43–46
Franzen, Ulrich, 83–84, 149
Fred and Ginger (Prague), 166–167
Freeman, George, 86
Fresnoy, Le, 175, 176
functional value, 11
Futurism, 179–181

Gehry, Frank, 166–167
Gibbs, James, 76
Gilbert, Cass, 39, 41, 42–43
Giurgola, Romaldo, 99–102, 120. *see also* Mitchell/Giurgola Architects
  Penn Mutual Life Insurance, 108–110
glass, 52–53
  Maison de Verre, 50–53
  Palais des Beaux Arts addition, 173–174
Göteborg law courts, 32–36
Gothic design, 46, 128, 171
Gothic Revival, 37, 88
Grand Central Terminal, 9, 17, 82, 83, 156–158
Graves, Michael, 151–153
Greene Hall, Columbia Law

School, 169–171
Greenwich Royal Naval Hospital. *see* Queen's House and Greenwich Royal Naval Hospital
Gropius, Walter, 17
Guggenheim Museum, 142–145
Guild House, 12
Gwathmey Siegel & Associates
  Guggenheim Museum addition, 142–145
  Princeton University restoration, 137–138
Hamilton, Alexander, 106
Hamilton Grange, 14
Hardy Holzman Pfeiffer Associates, 153–154, 155
Harkness Quadrangle, 17
Harrison, Wallace, 41, 119, 169, 170
Harrison & Abramovitz, 169
Harvard University, Harkness Quadrangle, 17
Haviland, John, 108
Hawksmoor, Nicholas, 96
Heinz & LaFarge, 128–130
Himmelbau, Coop, 48–49
History Faculty (Cambridge University), 177–179
Hopkins, Michael, 140–141
houses
  Hubertus House, 53–54
  Maison de Verre, 50–53
Howe, George, 169
Hubertus House, 53–54
humor, 42

Ibos and Vitart, 172–174
identity of buildings
  change in, 14
  in combined architecture, 14
  expression of, 11–12
  legal protection, 12–14, 79
  see also protected identity, 14
identity of place, 107
  legal recognition of, 11–12
imitation, 98, 161–163
ING Bank, 49–50
insertions, 137
International Style, 54, 96
IRCAM, 60–64
Isozaki, Arata, 122

Jackson, Andrew, 106
Jefferson, Thomas, 12, 103, 110–114
Jewett Arts Center, 171–172

Jewish Museum (New York), 162
Jewish Wing, Berlin Museum, 167
Johnson Gallery, Ellen, 39
Jones, Inigo, 21, 22, 25, 161

Kahn, Louis I.
  Center for British Art, 39
  Kimbell Art Museum, 98, 99
  Salk Institute, 110, 114–116
  Yale University Art Gallery, 36–39
Kansai airport, 12, 13
Kimbell Art Museum, 98, 99–102
Kleihues, Josef Paul, 43, 46–48
Koolhaas, Rem, 164

Lasdun, Denys, 125–126
La Jolla, California, 114
Lambs' Club, 85–86
Landmarks Preservation Law, 77, 78–84, 149
landscape, as design influence, 22–25
Las Vegas, Nevada, 163
Latrobe, Benjamin, 110
law
  conceptual basis of preservation law, 81, 158–159
  courthouse design, 32–36
  evolution of preservation law, 77–84, 158
  goals of preservation law, 77
  Grand Central Terminal addition, 9, 156–158
  objectivity in preservation judgments, 159
  protection of architectural identity in, 12–14
  worth of architecture in, 11–12
Lescaze, William, 122, 169
Lever House, 54–57
Levittown, 162–163
Libeskind, Daniel
  Jewish Wing, Berlin Museum, 167
  Victoria and Albert Museum, 168–169
Lille, France, 164, 172
Lingotto Conference Center, 179–181
London, England, 91, 95–98
  Bracken House, 140–141
  National Gallery, 135–136
  Number One Poultry Lane, 91, 96–98
  Victoria and Albert Museum, 168

Louvre, 67–70
Louvre Pyramid, 67–70
Lutyens, James, 96
Lyon, France, 164
  Cité Internationale, 31
  Opera House, 70–72
Lyon Opera House, 70–72

MacCormac, Richard, 125–126
Maderno, Carlo, 19, 21, 28, 29
Madison, James, 137
Magistero, Il, 139
Maitland Robinson Library, 104
Maison Carrée, 57–60
Maison de Verre, 50–53
Matthewson, Ernest J., 108
McKim, Mead & White, 110
  Brooklyn Museum of Art, 121–124
  Fairchild Center, Columbia University, 116–121
  Lambs' Club, 85–86
  Merchants' Exchange, 88–91
  Metropolitan Club, 155–156
  University of Virginia, 110–114
meaning in architecture
  interaction of new and old, 17–18, 32
meaning of architecture
  aesthetic foundation, 158–159
  conceptual basis of preservation law, 158–159, 161
  contemplation of uncertainty, 164–165
  context and, 107
  evaluating proposals for combined works, 85
  legal protection of, 12
  in modernism, 31–32
  objectivity in, 159
  protected identity, 91
  significance of, 161
  source of, 12, 105
  worth of, 11
Meier, Richard, 43–46
Merchants' Exchange, New York, 85, 88–91
Metropolitan Club (New York), 155–156
Metropolitan Museum of Art, 106
Michelangelo. see Buonarotti, Michelangelo
Mills, Robert, 110
Milunic, Vladimir, 166

Mitchell/Giurgola Architects, 120, 131–133
modernism, 15
  abstraction in, 31
  accomplishments, 31–32
  Eiffel tower as expression of, 31
  reactions against, 161
  successful combinations, 32
  successful derivations, 50–64
  successful extensions, 32–50
  successful transformations, 64–75
  in urban renewal, 78
Moneo, Rafael, 171–172
Morgan, J. P., 155
Mould, Jacob Wrey, 93
Museum of Decorative Arts, 43–46
Museum for Pre- and Early History, 43, 46–48
museums
  Carré d'Art, 57–60
  Castelvecchio, 25–29
  Davis Museum and Cultural Center, 171–172
  Jewish Wing, Berlin Museum, 167
  Museum for Pre- and Early History, 43, 46–48
  Museum of Decorative Arts, 43–46
  Victoria and Albert, 168–169
  Yale University Art Gallery, 36–39
  see also art galleries/museums
Mussolini, Benito, 21

National Gallery (London), 135–136
Naumberg Bandshell, 91–95
New Orleans, Louisiana, 79
New-York Historical Society, 153–154
New York Merchants' Exchange, 85, 88–91
New York, New York
  Cathedral Church of St. John the Divine, 128–130
  Dana Center, 98, 105
  Forty-second Street development, 128–130
  Grand Central Terminal, 9, 17, 82, 83, 156–158
  Guggenheim Museum, 142–145
  International Style buildings, 54
  Jewish Museum, 162
  Lambs' Club, 85–86
  Merchants' Exchange, 85, 88–91

Metropolitan Club, 155–156
Naumberg Bandshell, 91–95
New-York Historical Society, 153–154
Pepsi-Cola Building, 54–57
preservation law, 77, 78–84, 149, 158
South Street Seaport, 83–84, 147–151
Washington Court, 145–146
Whitney Museum of American Art, 151–153
Nîmes, France, 57
Nouvel, Jean, 70–72
Number One Poultry Lane, 96–98

Oberlin, Ohio, 39–43, 135, 169
Octagon, The, 131–133
office buildings
Bracken House, 140–141
Penn Mutual Life Insurance, 108–110
Pepsi-Cola Building, 54–57
Poultry Lane design, 91, 95–98
Olmstead & Vaux, 91, 105
ornamentation, 31

Palais des Beaux Arts (Lille), 172–174
Palladian architecture, 21–22
Palladio, Andrea, 22
Palmer & Hornbostel, 84
Pan Am building, 9, 157
Paris, France, 50–53
Centre Pompidou, 65–67
Grands Projets, 64–65
IRCAM, 60–64
Maison de Verre, 50–53
Peabody & Stearns, 87–88
Pei, I. M., 119, 157
Louvre pyramid, 67–70
Penn Mutual Life Insurance, 108–110
Pennsylvania Station, 9, 78, 158
Pepsi-Cola Building, 54–57, 85
Perrault, Claude, 67, 68
Peters, Wesley, 142
Philadelphia, Pennsylvania, 108
Piano, Renzo, 31–32
Centre Pompidou, 65–67
Cité Internationale, 31
IRCAM, 60–64
Kansai Airport, 12, 13
Lingotto Conference Center, 179–181

Pierre Hotel, 155, 156
plans, architectural
as master plans, 116–124
interpretation of, 110–116
Pokorny, Jan Hird, 147, 149
Polshek & Partners, James Stewart, 122
Brooklyn Museum of Art, 122
Columbia Law School addition, 169–171
Metropolitan Club addition, 155–156
Seamen's Church Institute, 147–151
Washington Court apartments, 145–146
Pompidou Centre, 60–64, 65–67
postmodernism, 161
Poultry Lane, London, 91, 95–98
Prague, Czech Republic, 166–167
Princeton University, 137–138
protected identity
architectural sources of, 105
conceptual basis of preservation law, 158–159
evaluation of proposed works, 15, 85
test for preservation, 85, 91
Protestant Reformation, 18
public value of architectural expression
challenges to preservation law, 81–82
in law, 11–12, 77, 81
source of, 11

Queen's House and Greenwich Royal Naval Hospital, 15, 18, 29, 161
design evolution, 21–25
landscape requirements, 22–25
significance of, 21

random design, 48
Reed & Stem, 157
Reichstag, 72–75, 175
Renaissance architecture, 18
representational architecture, 161, 162–163
Richardson, Albert, 140, 141
Richardson, H. H., 84
Rietveld, Gerrit, 14
Robie House, 142
Roche, Kevin, 162

Rockefeller Center, 169
Rockwell Museum, Norman, 161
Rogers, Isaiah, 88–91
Rogers, James Gamble, 118
Romanesque design, 128
Roth, Richard, 149
Rudolph, Paul, 39, 171–172

Saarinen, Eero, 164
Sainsbury Wing, National Gallery, 135–136
Saint John's College, 124, 126–128
Saint John the Divine, 128–130
Saint Martin's-in-the-Fields, 135
Saint Peter's Church, 15, 18, 29, 85
colonnade, 20
dome, 18, 19
door placement, 19
evolution, 18–21
façade, 19
physical center, 18
poché, 19
portico, 20
spiritual center, 19
St. Peter's tomb, 18–19, 20
Salk Institute, 110, 114–116
Scala, Can Grande della, 27, 28
Scarpa, Carlo, 25–28, 29, 161, 171
Schinkel, Karl Friedrich, 88
Schroeder House, 14
Seagram Building, 54–57
Seamen's Church Institute (New York), 147–151
Second Branch Bank on United States, 106
Seeler, Edgar J., 108
Serlio, 8
Sherman Fairchild Center for Life Sciences, 117–121
Silman, Robert, 161
Skidmore Owings Merrill, 54–57
Skull and Bones, 37
Snug Harbor, New York, 81–82
Soane, John Sir, 96
sociopolitical context
British brutalism, 124–125
Central Park preservation, 91
evolution of preservation law, 77–79, 81, 82
Hubertus House, 54
Louvre, 68–70
University of Virginia designs, 110–112
Wren's designs, 25

Soufflot, J. G., 70
South Street Seaport, New York, 83–84, 147–151
Staten Island, New York, 81–82
Stern, Robert A. M., 161
Stirling, James, 17, 135, 136, 160
    Cambridge University History Faculty, 177, 178–179
    Number One Poultry Lane design, 91, 95–98
Stockholm Library, 34
Street Hall, 37
Studio National des Arts Contemporains, 175–176
Swartwout, Egerton, 37

taking, legal concept of, 81
technology, 174–175
tectonic architecture, 174–175
Terry, Quinlan, 98, 103–104
Tessin, Nicodemus, 32
theoretical architecture, 164–165
Thompson, Martin, 106
Thompson Associates, Ben, 147
Thornton, William, 131
Tourcoing, France, 175
transformations, 64–75
Trumbull Gallery, 36
Tschumi, Bernard, 175–176
Turin, Italy, 140
    Lingotto Conference Center, 179–181
Turner, Frederick Jackson, 112
twentieth century, 15, 163–164. see also modernism preservation law, 77–85

United Nations, 170
United States Custom House, 85, 87–88
University of Virginia, 12, 110–114
urban renewal, 77–78
Urbino, Italy, 139

valuation of architecture
    conceptual basis, 11
    context, 17
    framework for, 9
    in law, 11–12, 84–85
    proposed combined works, 15
    recent combined works, 15
    twentieth century preservation law, 15, 77–85
van der Rohe, Mies, 96

van Eyck, Aldo, 53–54
Venturi, Robert, 31, 39–43, 75, 164. see also Venturi Rauch and Scott Brown
Venturi Rauch and Scott Brown, 135–136
Victoria and Albert Museum, 168–169
Vienna, Austria, 48–49
Vignoly, Raphael, 148

Walker & Gillette, 153
Wallot, Paul, 72
Walter, Thomas U., 10
Warren & Wetmore, 156–157
Washington, D.C., 34, 131
Washington Court apartments (New York), 145–146
Wellesley, Massachusetts, 171
Wexner Center for the Visual Arts, 164–166
Whig Hall (Princeton), 137–138
White, Stanford, 112
Whitney Museum of American Art, 151–153
Wight, P. B., 37
Wilkins, William, 103, 135, 136
wings, 131
Wingspread, 161
Woodland Crematorium, 35
worth of architecture, 11
Wren, Christopher, 21–25, 28, 29, 96, 161
Wright, Frank Lloyd, 42, 161
    Guggenheim Museum, 142
Wright, Stephen, 76, 105

Yale University, 36–39, 85
Yale University Art Gallery, 36–39
York & Sawyer, 153
Young, Ammi, 87